Whether you are encountering Italians in Italy or meeting them here,

whether you are facing a restaurant menu or a hotel desk clerk,

whether you are visiting a museum or stopping at a gas station,

whether you need directions or want to strike up a casual conversation,

whether you have to deal with a medical emergency or a mechanical breakdown,

whether you want to establish trust and good feelings in a business meeting or demonstrate warmth and courtesy in personal dealings, this one book is your

PASSPORT TO ITALIAN
New Revised Edition

NEW REVISED EDITION

CHARLES BERLITZ

PASSPORT TO

ITALIAN

Ⓢ
A SIGNET BOOK

SIGNET
Published by the Penguin Group
Penguin Books USA Inc., 375 Hudson Street,
New York, New York 10014, U.S.A.
Penguin Books Ltd, 27 Wrights Lane,
London W8 5TZ, England
Penguin Books Australia Ltd, Ringwood,
Victoria, Australia
Penguin Books Canada Ltd, 10 Alcorn Avenue,
Toronto, Ontario, Canada M4V 3B2
Penguin Books (N.Z.) Ltd, 182–190 Wairau Road,
Auckland 10, New Zealand

Penguin Books Ltd, Registered Offices:
Harmondsworth, Middlesex, England

First published by Signet, an imprint of Dutton Signet,
a division of Penguin Books USA Inc.

First Signet Printing, April, 1974
First Printing (Revised and Expanded Edition), April, 1986
First Printing (New Revised Edition), October, 1992
10 9 8 7 6

Printed in the United States of America

Contents

🐺 Preface

Passport to Italian is not a conventional phrase book, but rather a basis for conversing in and understanding Italian. The short sentences contain the key words and phrases most useful for travel, sight-seeing, visiting restaurants, shopping, business and, most importantly, for communicating with the Italians you may meet in Italy, Europe, and the Americas. You will be surprised and gratified by the friendly relations you establish when you take the trouble to address Italians in their melodious and beautiful language.

This book is designed to provide easy and instant communication. The phrases are short, pertinent to situations of daily life, and grouped for easy reference so that you can find the exact section you need at any moment.

Each phrase designed for your use on a trip to Italy is written first in English, then in Italian, and finally in easy-to-pronounce phonetics. When the Italian word has a syllable that must be stressed, this syllable is written in capitals, which will give an authentic tone to your accent and helps Italians to understand you easily.

To facilitate a mutual understanding we have added special sections to certain chapters. These are called *POINT TO THE ANSWER*. Here the first sentence is in Italian with the English written below. A note in Italian requests the person to whom you are speaking to point to the answer to your specific question with the result that you not only understand the reply but obtain additional practice in learning how Italian sounds without relying on the English phonetics in most other chapters. This is an assured practice method that will give you added confidence and improve your accent through communicating in Italian with an Italian person.

The use of this book will more than double your enjoyment of a trip abroad, avoid misunderstanding—financial or otherwise—and help you save money. Besides the economic factor, why visit a foreign country if you can't break the language barrier and communicate with the new and interesting people you meet? You might as well stay home and see the palaces and monuments of the country on color TV. And in any case, who wants to be limited to one language when picking up another can be so easy and enjoyable?

One can speak and understand current everyday Italian with comparatively few words and phrases—perhaps 1,500 to 1,800—which is less than the number given in the special dictionary at the end of this book. By using the same short constructions over and over, in the various situations where they normally occur, you will learn them without conscious effort. They will become a part of your own vocabulary and of your memory bank, and that is, after all, the only secret of learning a language.

How to Acquire an Instant Italian Accent

Every word or sentence in this book is printed first in English, then in Italian, then in an easy-to-say pronunciation system to help you to pronounce the Italian.

Just read the third line as if you were reading English and stress the syllables written in capital letters.

English: **Do you speak Italian?**
Italian: Parla Lei italiano?
Pronunciation: *PAR-la lay ee-tahl-YA-no?*

Although the following points are made clear in the third line, they will be helpful for you in pronouncing and reading Italian generally.

The vowels **a, e, i, o** and **u** are always pronounced *ah, eh, ee, oh, oo*. In our pronunciation system we have added an *h* to some syllables, such as *do* and *to*, to remind you to pronounce them *doh* and *toh* and not like the English words "do" and "to."

c before **e** or **i** is pronounced like English *ch*; otherwise, it is pronounced *k*.

ch is pronounced like *k*.

g before **e** or **i** is pronounced as in the English "general"; otherwise as in "gave."

gh is pronounced like the *gh* in "spaghetti."

gl is pronounced like the *lli* in "million."

gn is pronounced like the *ny* in "canyon."

h is silent.

s is pronounced like an English *z* when it comes between the vowels.

sc before **e** or **i** is pronounced like English *sh*; otherwise, it is pronounced *sk*.

sch is pronounced *sk*.

z is pronounced *dz* at the beginning of the word, and generally *ts* within a word.

zz is pronounced like *ts* and occasionally like *dz*.

1. Greetings and Introductions

When addressing people call them **Signore, Signora**, or **Signorina**, with or *without* adding their last names. Even when you say simply **Buongiorno**, it is more polite to add one of these titles to it:

Mr. (or) **Sir**	**Mrs.** (or) **Madam**	**Miss**
Signore	Signora	Signorina
seen-YO-reh	*seen-YO-ra*	*seen-yo-REE-na*

Good morning (or) **Good day** (or) **Good afternoon, sir.**
Buongiorno, signore.
bwohn-JOR-no, seen-YO-reh.

Good evening, miss.
Buono sera, signorina.
BWO-na SAIR-ra, seen-yo-REE-na.

How are you?
Come sta?
KO-meh sta?

Very well, thank you. And you?
Molto bene, grazie. E Lei?
MOHL-toh BEH-neh, GRAHTS-yeh. eh lay?

Come in.
Avanti.
ah-VAHN-tee.

Make yourself comfortable.
Si accomodi, prego.
see ahk-KO-mo-dee, PREH-go.

Your name, please?
Il Suo nome, prego?
eel SOO-wo NO-meh, PREH-go?

I am Charles Dinardo.
Io sono Carlo Dinardo.
EE-yo SO-no KAR-lo dee-NAR-doh.

May I present Mr. _____
Le presento Signor _____
le preh-ZEN-toh seen-YOR _____

Delighted to meet you.
Piacere.
P'ya-CHEH-reh.

1

Where are you from?
Di dov'è Lei?
dee doh-VEH lay?

I am American.
Sono americano.
SOH-no ah-meh-ree-KA-no.

My wife is Italian.
Mia moglie è italiana.
MEE-ya MOHL-yeh eh ee-tahl-YA-na.

What city are you from?
Di che città è Lei?
dee keh chee-TA eh lay?

Is it your first trip here?
E il Suo primo viaggio qui?
eh eel SOO-wo PREE-mo V'YA-jo kwee?

Have a nice time in Italy!
Che si diverta in Italia!
keh see dee-VEHR-ta een ee-TAHL-ya!

(You are) Very kind.
Molto gentile.
MOHL-toh jen-TEE-leh.

Good-bye. (formal)
ArrivederLa.
ah-ree-veh-DEHR-la.

Good-bye. (less formal)
Arrivederci.
ah-ree-veh-DEHR-chee.

Hi! (or) **So long!**
Ciao!
chow!

A proposito (By the way): When you say "Mr." with a man's last name, **signore** is shortened to **signor**. Mr. Dinardo—**Signor Dinardo. Signora** and **signorina** do not change.

2. Basic Expressions

Learn these by heart. You will use them every time you speak Italian to someone. If you memorize these expressions and the numbers in the next section you will find that you can ask prices, directions, and generally make your wishes known.

Yes.	**No.**	**Perhaps.**	**Of course.**
Sí.	No.	Forse.	Certamente.
see.	*no.*	*FOR-seh.*	*chair-ta-MEN-teh.*

Please.	**Thank you.**	**You are welcome.**
Per piacere.	Grazie.	Prego.
pair p'ya-CHEH-reh.	*GRAHTS-yeh.*	*PREH-go.*

Excuse me.	**I'm sorry.**	**It's all right.**
Mi scusi.	Mi dispiace.	Va bene.
mee SKOO-zee.	*mee dees-P'YA-cheh.*	*va BEH-neh.*

Here.	**There.**	**This.**	**That.**
Qui.	Là.	Questo.	Quello.
kwee.	*la.*	*KWESS-toh.*	*KWEL-lo.*

Do you speak English?	**I speak Italian a little.**
Parla inglese?	Parlo un po' d'italiano.
PAR-la een-GLEH-zeh?	*PAR-lo oon po dee-tahl-YA-no.*

Do you understand?	**I understand.**
Capisce?	Capisco.
ka-PEE-sheh?	*ka-PEE-sko.*

I don't understand.	**Very well.**
Non capisco.	Molto bene.
nohn ka-PEE-sko.	*MOHL-toh BEH-neh.*

When?
Quando?
KWAHN-doh?

How far?
Quanto è lontano?
KWAHN-toh eh lohn-TA-no?

How much time?
Quanto tempo?
KWAHN-toh TEM-po?

How?
Come?
KO-meh?

Why not?
Perchè no?
pair-KEH no?

Like this.
Così.
ko-ZEE.

Not like that.
Non così.
nohn ko-ZEE.

It is possible.
È possibile.
eh pohs-SEE-bee-leh.

It is not possible.
Non è possibile.
Nohn eh pohs-SEE-bee-leh.

Now.
Adesso.
ah-DEHS-so.

Not now.
Non adesso.
nohn al-DEHS-so.

Later.
Più tardi.
p'yoo TAR-dee.

That's fine.
Va bene.
va BEH-neh.

It's very good.
È molto buono.
eh MOHL-toh BWO-no.

It's not good.
Non è buono.
nohn eh BWO-no.

It's very important.
È molto importante.
eh MOHL-toh eem-por-TAHN-teh.

It doesn't matter.
Non importa.
nohn eem-POR-ta.

Speak slowly, please.
Parli piano, per favore.
PAR-lee P'YA-no, pair fa-VO-reh.

Repeat, please.
Ripeta, per favore.
ree-PEH-ta, pair fa-VO-reh.

Write it.
Lo scriva.
lo SKREE-va.

Who is it?
Chi è?
kee eh?

Come in.
Avanti.
ah-VAHN-tee.

Don't come in.
Non entri.
nohn EN-tree.

Stop.
Si fermi.
see FAIR-mee.

Wait.
Aspetti.
ah-SPET-tee.

Let's go.
Andiamo.
ahn-D'YA-mo.

That's all.
È tutto.
eh TOOT-toh.

What is this?
Che cos'è questo?
keh ko-ZEH KWES-toh?

Where is the telephone?
Dov'è il telefono?
doh-VEH eel teh-LEH-fo-no?

Where is the restroom?
Dov'è la toeletta?
doh-VEH la toh-eh-LET-ta?

. . . for ladies?
. . . per donne?
. . . pair DOHN-neh?

. . . for men?
. . . per signori?
. . . pair seen-YO-ree?

Show me.
Mi mostri.
mee MO-stree.

How much?
Quanto?
KWAHN-toh?

It's too much.
È troppo.
eh TROHP-po.

Isn't it?
Non è vero?
nohn eh VEH-ro?

Who?
Chi?
kee?

I
io
EE-yo

you (singular)
Lei
lay

you (plural)
Loro (or) voi
LO-ro (or) voy

he
egli
EHL-yee

she
ella
EL-la

we
noi
noy

they
essi, esse
EHS-see, EHS-say

A proposito: You can always use **per favore**, which means "please" or, literally, "as a favor," when you ask questions or make requests. It can also function for "Bring me," "I want," or "I would like." Simply say **per favore** followed by the word for whatever you want, which you can find in the dictionary section.

Non è vero? can be used to request agreement to something or to mean "Isn't it?" "Isn't that right?" or "Don't you think so?"

Italian nouns and adjectives generally end in -o for masculine words and -a for feminine ones. Ex.: *italiano, italiana; americano, americana.*

🐺 3. Numbers

The numbers are important not only for asking prices (and perhaps to bargain) but also for phone numbers, addresses, and telling time. Learn the first twenty by heart and then from 20 to 100 by tens, and you can deal with **danaro** (money), **un numero di telefono** (a telephone number), **un indirizzo** (an address), and **l'ora** ("the hour," in telling time).

1	2	3	4	5
uno	due	tre	quattro	cinque
OO-no	*DOO-weh*	*treh*	*KWAHT-tro.*	*CHEEN-kweh*

6	7	8	9	10
sei	sette	otto	nove	dieci
say	*SET-teh*	*OHT-toh*	*NO-veh*	*D'YEH-chee*

11	12	13
undici	dodici	tredici
OON-dee-chee	*DOH-dee-chee*	*TREH-dee-chee*

14	15	16
quattordici	quindici	sedici
kwaht-TOR-dee-chee	*KWEEN-dee-chee*	*SEH-dee-chee*

17	8	19
diciassette	diciotto	diciannove
DEE-chahs-SET-teh	*dee-CHOHT-toh*	*dee-chahn-NO-veh*

20	21	22
venti	ventuno	ventidue
VAIN-tee	*vain-TOO-no*	*vain-tee-DOO-weh*

23	24	25
ventitrè	ventiquattro	venticinque
vain-tee-TREH	*vain-tee KWAHT-tro*	*vain-tee-CHEEN-kweh*

7

30	40	50	60
trenta	quaranta	cinquanta	sessanta
TRAIN-ta	*kwa-RAHN-ta*	*cheen-KWAHN-ta*	*sehs-SAHN-ta*

70	80	90	100
settanta	ottanta	novanta	cento
set-TAHN-ta	*oht-TAHN-ta*	*no-VAHN-ta*	*CHEN-toh*

200	300	400
duecento	trecento	quattrocento
doo-weh-CHEN-toh	*treh-CHEN-toh*	*kwaht-tro-CHEN-toh*

500	600	700
cinquecento	seicento	settecento
cheen-kweh-CHEN-toh	*say-CHEN-toh*	*set-teh-CHEN-toh*

800	900
ottocento	novecento
oht-toh-CHEN-toh	*no-veh-CHEN-toh*

1000	2000	3000
mille	due mila	tre mila
MEEL-leh	*DOO-weh MEE-la*	*treh MEE-la*

100,000	1,000,000
cento mila	un milione
CHEN-toh MEE-la	*oon meel-YO-neh*

1st	2nd	3rd
primo	secondo	terzo
PREE-mo	*seh-KOHN-doh*	*TAIRT-so*

last
ultimo
OOL-tee-mo

half
mezzo
MED-zo

zero
zero
DZEH-ro

How much?
Quanto?
KWAHN-toh?

How many?
Quanti?
KWAHN-tee?

What number?
Che numero?
keh NOO-meh-ro?

🐺 4. Arrival

Besides talking to airport officials, one of the most important things you will need to do on arrival in Italy is to find your way around. For this reason we offer you here some basic "asking-your-way" questions and answers and call your attention to the "Point to the Answer" sections, which the people to whom you speak can use to *point out* answers to make it easier for you to understand.

Passport, please.
Passaporto, prego.
pahs-sa-POR-toh, PREH-go.

I am on a visit.
Sono di passaggio.
SO-no dee pahs-SAHJ-jo.

For three weeks.
Per tre settimane.
Pair treh set-tee-MA-neh.

I am on a business trip.
Sono in viaggio d'affari.
SO-no in V'YAHD-jo dahf-FA-ree.

Where is the customs?
Dov'è la dogana?
doh-VEH la doh-GA-na?

Where is the baggage?
Dov'è il bagaglio?
doh-VEH eel ba-GAHL-yo?

Flight 40.
Volo numero quaranta.
VO-lo NOO-meh-ro kwa-RAHN-ta.

Over there.
Laggiù.
LAHD-joo.

This one is mine.
Questa è mia.
KWESS-ta eh MEE-ya.

That one.
Quella.
KWEL-la.

Shall I open it?
Devo aprire?
DEH-vo ah-PREE-reh?

Open it.
Apra.
AH-pra.

11

One moment, please.
Un momento, per piacere.
oon mo-MEHN-toh, pair p'ya-CHEH-reh.

There you are.
Ecco.
EHK-ko.

I have nothing to declare.
Non ho niente da dichia-rare.
nohn oh N'YEN-teh da deek-ya-RA-reh.

This has been used.
Questo è usato.
KWEH-sto eh oo-ZA-roh.

These are for my personal use.
Sono oggetti personali.
SO-no oh-JET-tee pair-so-NA-lee.

These are gifts.
Sono regali.
SO-no reh-GA-lee.

Where is a telephone?
Dov'è un telefono?
doh-VEH oon teh-LEH-fo-no?

. . . a taxi stand?
. . . un posteggio di tassì?
. . . oon po-STEJ-jo dee tahs-SEE?

Where is the bus to the city?
Dov'è l'autobus per la città?
doh-VEH L'OW-toh-booss pair la cheet-TA?

Where is a restaurant?
Dov'è un ristorante?
doh-VEH oon ree-sto-RAHN-teh?

Where is the rest room?
Dov'è la toeletta?
doh-VEH la toh-eh-LET-ta?

Porter!
Facchino!
fahk-KEE-no!

Take these to a taxi.
Porti queste a un tassì.
POR-tee KWEH-steh ah oon tahs-SEE.

I'll carry this one myself.
Questa la porto io.
KWEH-sta la POR-toh EE-yo.

Taxi, are you free?
Tassi, è libero?
tahs-SEE, eh LEE-beh-ro?

To the Hotel Gritti.
All'Albergo Gritti.
ahl-lahl-BAIR-go GREET-
tee.

How much is it?
Quant'è?
kwahn-TEH?

To the Villa Medici.
Alla Villa Medici.
AHL-la VEEL-la MEH-dee-chee.

Excuse me, how can I go . . .
Mi scusi, che strada faccio per andare . . .
mee SKOO-zee, keh STRA-da FA-cho pair ahn-DA-
reh . . .

. . . to a good restaurant?
. . . a un buon ristorante?
. . . ah oon bwohn ree-sto-RAHN-teh?

. . . to the American Consulate?
. . . al consolato americano?
. . . ahl kohn-so-LA-toh ah-meh-ree-KA-no?

. . . English?
. . . inglese?
. . . een-GLEH-zeh?

. . . Canadian?
. . . canadese?
. . . ka-na-DEH-zeh?

. . . to this address?
. . . a quest'indirizzo?
. . . ah kwehst-een-dee-
REET-tso?

. . . to the movies?
. . . al cinema?
. . . ahl CHEE-neh-ma?

. . . to the post office?
. . , alla posta?
. . . AHL-la PO-sta?

. . . to a police station?
. . . alla polizia?
. . . AHL-la po-leet-SEE-ya?

. . . to a pharmacy?
. . . a uno farmacia?
. . . ah OO-na far-ma-
CHEE-ya?

. . . to a hospital?
. . . a un ospedale?
. . . ah oon oh-speh-DA-leh?

. . . to a barber?
. . . da un barbiere?
. . . *da oon barb-YEH-reh?*

. . . to a hairdresser?
. . . da un parrucchiere?
. . . *da oon par-rook-YEH-reh?*

. . . to a department store?
. . . ad un grande magazzino?
. . . *ahd oon GRAHN-deh ma-gahd-T'SEE-no?*

Thank you very much.
Grazie tante.
GRAHTS-yeh TAHN-teh.

You are very kind.
Molto gentile.
MOHL-toh jen-TEE-leh.

A proposito: When you speak to a stranger, don't forget to say **Mi scusi, signore** (or **signora** or **signorina**) before you ask a question. If you speak to a policeman, call him **Guardia** (GWAHRD-ya).

Streets in Italy have signs on the buildings at each corner, making it easy to find out where you are.

To make sure you understand people's answers you can show them the "Point to the Answer" section following.

POINT TO THE ANSWER

To make sure that you understand the answer to a question, show the following section to the Italian person you are talking to so that he or she can select the answer. The sentence in Italian after the arrow asks the person to point to the answer to your question.

 La prego di mostrare qui sotto la Sua risposta alla mia domanda. Molte grazie.

È da quella parte.
It's that way.

Su via _____.
On _____ avenue.

A destra.   **A sinistra.**   **Diritto.**
To the right.   To the left.   Straight ahead.

È vicino.   **Si può andare.**
It's near.   You can walk.

È lontano.   **Prenda un tassì.**
It's far.   Take a taxi.

Prenda l'autobus.   **All'angolo.**
Take the bus.   On the corner.

Scenda a _____.
Get off at _____.

You will find other "Point to the Answer" sections on pages
23, 36, 44, 46, 49, 56, 60, 70, 98, and a special condensed
"Point to the Answer" section starting on page *223*.

5. Hotel—Laundry—
Dry Cleaning

Although the staffs of the larger hotels have some training in
English, you will find that the use of Italian makes for better
understanding and better relations, especially with the service
personnel. Besides, it's fun, and you should practice Italian
at every opportunity. We have included laundry and dry
cleaning in this section, as this is one of the things for which
you have to make yourself understood in speaking to the
hotel chambermaid or valet.

Can you recommend a good hotel?
Può raccomandarmi un buon albergo?
pwo rahk-ko-mahn-DAR-mee oon bwohn ahl-BAIR-go?

. . . a guest house?
. . . una pensione?
. . . OO-na pens-YO-neh?

. . . in the center of town.
. . . nel centro.
. . . nel CHEN-tro.

At a reasonable price.
A buon prezzo.
ah bwohn PREHT-tso.

I have a reservation.
Ho prenotato.
oh preh-no-TA-toh.

My name is _____
Mi chiamo _____
mee K'YA-mo _____

Have you a room?
Ha una stanza?
ah OO-na STAHNT-sa?

I would like a room . . .
Vorrei una stanza . . .
*vor-RAY OO-na STAHNT-
sa . . .*

. . . for one person.
. . . per una persona.
. . . pair OO-na pair-SO-na.

. . . for two people.
. . . per due persone.
*. . . pair DOO-weh pair-SO-
neh.*

. . . with two beds.
. . . con due letti.
*. . . kohn DOO-weh LET-
tee.*

. . . with a bathroom.
. . . con bagno.
. . . *kohn BAHN-yo.*

. . . with hot water.
. . . con acqua calda.
. . . *kohn AH-kwa KAHL-da.*

. . . air-conditioned.
. . . con aria condizionata.
. . . *kohn AHR-ya kohn-deets-yo-NA-ta.*

. . . with a radio.
. . . con radio.
. . . *kohn RAHD-yo.*

. . . with television.
. . . con televisione.
. . . *kohn teh-leh-veez-YO-neh.*

. . . with a terrace.
. . . con terrazza.
. . . *kohn tehr-RAHT-tsa.*

Two communicating rooms.
Due stanze comunicanti.
DOO-weh STAHNT-seh ko-moo-nee-KAHN-tee.

How much is it?
Quanto costa?
KWAHN-toh KO-sta?

. . . per day?
. . . al giorno?
. . . *ahl JOR-no?*

. . . per week?
. . . alla setti-
mana?
. . . *AHL-la set-tee-MA-na?*

Are the meals included?
Pranzo compreso?
PRAHNT-so kohm-PREH-zo?

Is breakfast included?
Colazione compresa?
ko-lahts-YO-neh kohm-PREH-za?

I should like to see it.
Vorrei vederla.
vor-RAY veh-DAIR-la.

Where is the bath?
Dov'è il bagno?
doh-VEH eel BAHN-yo?

. . . the shower?
. . . la doccia?
. . . *la DOHT-cha?*

I want another room.
Vorrei un'altra stanza.
*vor-RAY oon AHL-tra
STAHNT-sa.*

. . . higher up.
. . . più in alto.
. . . p'yoo in AHL-toh.

. . . better.
. . . migliore.
. . . meel-YO-reh.

. . . larger.
. . . più grande.
*. . . p'yoo
GRAHN-deh.*

. . . smaller.
. . . più piccola.
*. . . p'yoo PEEK-
ko-la.*

I'll take this room.
Prendo questa.
PREN-doh KWESS-ta

I'll stay for five days.
Resterò per cinque giorni.
*ress-teh-RO pair CHEEN-
kweh JOR-nee.*

What is checkout time?
A che ora si deve lasciare la stanza?
ah keh OH-ra see DEH-veh la-SHA-reh la STAHNT-sa?

What time is lunch served?
A che ora è servita la colazione?
ah keh OH-ra eh sair-VEE-ta la ko-lahts-YO-neh?

What time is dinner served?
A che ora è servito il pranzo?
ah keh OH-ra eh sair-VEE-toh eel PRAHNT-so?

I would like a bottle of mineral water and ice.
Vorrei una bottiglia d'acqua minerale con ghiaccio.
*vor-RAY OO-na boht-TEEL-ya DAHK-wa mee-neh-RA-
leh kohn G'YAHT-cho.*

Send breakfast to room number 109.
Mandi la colazione alla stanza numero 109.
*MAHN-dee la ko-lahts-YO-neh AHL-la STAHNT-sa
NOO-meh-ro CHEN-toh-NO-veh.*

Orange juice, coffee with milk, rolls and butter.*
Succo d'arancia, caffè con latte, pane e burro.
SOOK-ko da-RAHN-cha, kahf-FEH kohn LAHT-teh, PA-neh eh BOOR-ro.

Will you send these letters for me?
Può spedire queste lettere per me?
pwo speh-DEE-reh KWEH-steh LET-teh-reh pair meh?

Will you put stamps on them?
Può mettere i francobolli?
pwo MET-teh-reh ee frahn-ko-BOHL-lee?

The key, please.
La chiave, per favore.
la K'YA-veh, pair fa-VO-reh.

Is there any mail for me?
C'è posta per me?
cheh PO-sta pair meh?

Send my mail to this address.
Mandi le mie lettere a quest'indirizzo.
MAHN-dee leh MEE-yeh LET-teh-reh ah kwest een-dee-REET-tso.

I want to speak to the manager.
Vorrei parlare con il direttore.
vor-RAY par-LA-reh kohn eel dee-ret-TOH-reh.

I need an interpreter.
Ho bisogno di un interprete.
oh bee-ZOHN-yo dee oon een-TAIR-preh-teh.

Are you the chambermaid?
È Lei la cameriera?
eh lay la ka-mair-YEH-ra?

---

*For a more complete breakfast see page 31.

I need . . .
Ho bisogno di . . .
oh bee-ZOHN-yo dee . . .

. . . a blanket.
. . . una coperta.
. . . OO-na ko-PAIR-ta.

. . . a pillow.
. . . un cuscino.
. . . oon koo-SHEE-no.

. . . a towel.
. . . un asciugamano.
. . . oon ah-shoo-ga-MA-no.

. . . soap.
. . . sapone.
. . . sa-PO-neh.

. . . toilet paper.
. . . carta igienica.
. . . KAR-ta ee-JEH-nee-ka.

This is to be dry-cleaned.
Questo è da lavare a secco.
KWESS-toh eh da la-VA-reh ah SEK-ko.

This is to be pressed.
Questo è da stirare.
KWESS-toh eh da stee-RA-reh.

This is to be washed.
Questo è da lavare.
KWESS-toh eh da la-VA-reh.

This is to be repaired.
Questo è da riparare.
KWESS-toh eh da ree-pa-RA-reh.

For this evening?
Per questa sera?
pair KWESS-ta SEH-ra?

. . . tomorrow?
. . . domani?
. . . doh-MA-nee?

. . . tomorrow afternoon?
. . . domani pomeriggio?
. . . doh-MA-nee po-meh-REED-jo?

. . . tomorrow evening?
. . . domani sera?
. . . doh-MA-nee SEH-ra?

When?
Quando?
KWAHN-doh?

For sure?
Di sicuro?
dee see-KOO-ro?

Be careful with this.
Faccia attenzione con questo.
FAHT-cha aht-tents-YO-neh kohn KWESS-toh.

Don't press this with a hot iron.
Non stiri questo con il ferro caldo.
nohn STEE-ree KWESS-toh kohn eel FAIR-ro KAHL-doh.

The dry cleaner.
La tintoria.
la teen-toh-REE-ya.

Are my clothes ready?
Sono pronto i miei vestiti?
so-no PROHN-tee ee M'YAY ves-TEE-tee?

Prepare my bill, please.
Mi prepari il conto, per piacere.
mee preh-PA-ree eel KOHN-toh, pair p'ya-CHEH-reh.

I'm leaving tomorrow morning.
Parto domani mattina.
PAR-to doh-MA-nee maht-TEE-na.

Can you call me at seven o'clock?
Mi può chiamare alle sette?
mee pwo k'ya-MA-reh AHL-leh SET-teh?

It's very important.
È molto importante.
eh MOHL-toh eem-por-TAHN-teh.

A proposito: Hotel floors are generally counted starting above the ground floor—**pianterreno**—so that the second floor is called the first, the third the second, etc.

You don't have to ask for a shoeshine at a hotel. Just leave your shoes outside the door as you retire. Not a bad idea, **non è vero?** (Isn't that so?)

POINT TO THE ANSWER

To make sure that you understand the answer to a question, show the following section to the Italian person you are talking to so that he or she can select the answer. The sentence in Italian after the arrow asks him or her to point to the answer to your question.

 La prego di mostrare qui sotto la Sua risposta alla mia domanda. Molte grazie!

Oggi.
Today.

Stasera.
This evening.

Domani.
Tomorrow.

Presto.
Early.

Tardi.
Late.

Nel pomeriggio.
In the afternoon.

Prima dell'una.
Before one o'clock.

Prima delle due, tre, quattro, cinque.
Before two, three, four, five o'clock.

All'una.
At one o'clock.

Alle sei, sette, otto, nove, dieci, undici, dodici.
At six, seven, eight, nine, ten, eleven, twelve o'clock.

lunedì
Monday

martedì
Tuesday

mercoledì
Wednesday

giovedì
Thursday

venerdì
Friday

sabato
Saturday

domenica
Sunday

6. Time: Hours—Days— Months

In the "Hotel" chapter you noted that when making an appointment at a certain hour you simply put **alle** in front of the number, except for "one o'clock," when you use **all'**. The following section shows you how to tell time in greater detail, including dates. You can make all sorts of arrangements with people by indicating the hour, the day, the date, and adding the phrase **Va bene?**—"Is that all right?"

What time is it?
Che ora è?
keh OH-ra eh?

It is one o'clock.
È l'una.
eh LOO-na.

It is six o'clock.
Sono le sei.
SO-no leh say.

Half past six.
Le sei e mezzo.
leh say eh MED-dzo.

A quarter past seven.
Le sette e un quarto.
leh SET-teh eh oon KWAR-toh.

A quarter to eight.
Le otto meno un quarto.
leh OHT-toh MEH-no oon KWAR-toh.

Ten minutes past ten.
Le dieci e dieci.
leh D'YEH-chee eh D'YEH-chee.

Ten minutes to three.
Le tre meno dieci.
Leh treh MEH-no D'YEH-chee.

At nine o'clock.
Alle nove.
AHL-leh NO-veh.

At exactly nine o'clock.
Alle nove in punto.
AHL-leh NO-veh een POON-toh.

in the morning.
di mattina
dee maht-TEE-na

in the afternoon
di pomeriggio
dee po-meh-REED-jo

25

in the evening
di sera
dee SEH-ra

at night
di notte
dee NOHT-teh

today
oggi
OHD-jee

tomorrow
domani
doh-MA-nee

yesterday
ieri
YEH-ree

the day after tomorrow
dopodomani
doh-po-doh-MA-nee

the day before yesterday
ieri l'altro
YEH-ree LAHL-tro

this evening
questa sera
KWESS-ta SEH-ra

last night
ieri sera
YEH-ree SEH-ra

tomorrow evening
domani sera
doh-MA-nee SEH-ra

this week
questa settimana
KWESS-ta set-tee-MA-na

last week
la settimana scorsa
la set-tee-MA-na SKOR-sa

next week
la settimana prossima
*la set-tee-MA-na PROHS-see-
ma*

two weeks ago
due settimane fa
DOO-weh set-tee-MA-neh fa

this month
questo mese
KWESS-toh MEH-zeh

last year
l'anno passato
LAHN-no pahs-SA-toh

next year
l'anno prossimo
LAHN-no PROHS-see mo

five years ago
cinque anni fa
CHEEN-kweh AHN-nee fa

1990
millenovecentonovanta
*MEEL-leh-no-veh-CHEN-
toh-no-VAHN-ta*

Monday
lunedì
loo-neh-DEE

Tuesday
martedì
mar-teh-DEE

Wednesday
mercoledì
mair-ko-leh-DEE

Thursday	**Friday**	**Saturday**	**Sunday**
giovedì	venerdì	sabato	domenica
jo-veh-DEE	*veh-nair-DEE*	*SA-ba-toh*	*doh-MEH-nee-ka*

next Monday
lunedì prossimo
loo-neh-DEE PROHS-see-mo

last Tuesday
martedì scorso
mar-teh-DEE SKOR-so

on Fridays
il venerdì
eel veh-nair-DEE

every Monday
ogni lunedì
OHN-yee loo-neh-DEE

January	**February**	**March**
gennaio	febbraio	marzo
jen-NA-yo	*feb-BRA-yo*	*MART-so*

April	**May**	**June**
aprile	maggio	giugno
ah-PREE-leh	*MAHD-jo*	*JOON-yo*

July	**August**	**September**
luglio	agosto	settembre
LOOL-yo	*ah-GO-sto*	*set-TEM-breh*

October	**November**	**December**
ottobre	novembre	dicembre
oht-TOH-breh	*no-VEM-breh*	*dee-CHEM-breh*

What date?
Che data?
keh DA-ta?

March 1st
il primo marzo
eel PREE-mo MART-so

March 2nd	**3rd**	**4th**
il due di marzo	il tre	il quattro
eel DOO-weh dee MART-so	*eel treh*	*eel KWAHT-tro*

the 25th of December
il venticinque di dicembre
*eel vain-tee-CHEEN-kweh
dee dee-CHEM-breh*

Merry Christmas!
Buon Natale!
bwohn na-TA-leh!

the 1st of January
il primo gennaio
eel PREE-mo jen-NA-yo

Happy New Year!
Buon Anno!
bwohn AHN-no!

Happy Birthday!
Buon compleanno!
bwohn cohm-pleh-AHN-no!

Congratulations!
Auguri!
ow-GOO-ree!

the 15th of August
il quindici d'agosto
*eel KWEEN-dee-chee da-
GO-sto*

(Have a) good vacation!
Buone vacanze!
BWO-neh va-KAHN-dzeh!

A proposito: The 15th of August is called **ferragosto**, traditionally a day for starting one's vacation.

Italians also celebrate many feast days of particular saints—each one called **la festa di San** ——— (or **Santa** ———) followed by the saint's name. These **feste** are often marked by colorful and interesting processions.

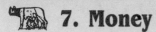 # 7. Money

This section contains the vocabulary necessary for handling money. Italian bills come in denominations of 1,000, 5,000, 10,000, 50,000 and 100,000 lire. Also there are coins in smaller values of lire.

Where can I change money?
Dove posso cambiare soldi?
DOH-veh POHS-so kahm-B'YA-reh SOHL-dee?

Can I change dollars here?
Posso cambiare dei dollari qui?
POHS-so kahm-B'YA-reh day DOHL-la-ree kwee?

Where is a bank?
Dove c'è una banca?
DOH-veh cheh OO-na BAHN-ka?

What time does the bank open?
A che ora si apre la banca?
ah keh OH-ra see AH-preh la BAHN-ka?

At what time does it close?
A che ora si chiude?
ah keh OH-ra see K'YOO-deh?

What's the dollar rate?
A quanto è il dollaro?
ah KWAHN-toh eh eel DOHL-la-ro?

Six hundred and twenty lire for one dollar.
Seicento venti lire al dollaro.
say-CHEN-toh VAIN-tee LEE-reh ahl DOHL-la-ro.

I want to change $50.
Voglio cambiare cinquanta dollari.
VOHL-yo kahm-B'YA-reh cheen-KWAHN-ta DOHL-la-ree.

Do you accept travelers checks?
Accetta assegni turistici?
aht-CHET-ta ahs-SEN-yee too-REE-stee-chee?

Of course.
Certamente.
chair-ta-MEN-teh.

Sorry; not here.
Mi dispiace; non qui.
mee dees-P'YA-cheh; non kwee.

Will you accept my check?
Accetta un mio assegno?
aht-CHET-ta oon MEE-yo ahs-SEN-yo?

Have you identification?
Ha documenti d'identità?
ah doh-koo-MEN-tee dee-den-tee-TA?

Yes, here is my passport.
Sì, ecco il mio passaporto.
see, EK-ko eel MEE-yo pahs-sa-POR-toh.

Give me two bills of ten thousand . . .
Prego mi dia due biglietti da diecimila . . .
preh-go mee DEE-ya DOO-weh beel-YET-tee da d'yeh-chee-MEE-la . . .

. . . four of five thousand and ten of a thousand
. . . quattro da cinquemila e dieci da mille
. . KWAHT-tro da CHEEN-kweh-MEE-la eh D'YEH-chee da MEE-leh

I need some small change.
Ho bisogno di spiccioli.
oh bee-ZOHN-yo dee SPEET-cho-lee.

8. Basic Foods

The foods and drinks mentioned in this section will enable you to be well fed, and in Italy that is very well indeed! The section that follows this will deal with special Italian dishes, representative of the **cucina**—"art of cooking"—that is one of the many and outstanding products of Italian culture.

breakfast
colazione
ko-lahts-YO-neh

orange juice
succo d'arancia
SOOK-ko da-RAHN-cha

grapefruit
pompelmo
pohm-PEL-mo

soft-boiled eggs
uova alla coque
WO-va AHL-la kohk

fried eggs
uova all'occhio
WO-va ahl-LOHK-k'yo

an omelet
una frittata
OO-na freet-TA-ta

scrambled eggs
uova strapazzate
WO-va stra-paht-TSA-teh

. . . with bacon
. . . con lardo
. . . *kohn LAR-doh*

. . . with ham
. . . con prosciutto
. . . *kohn pro-SHOOT-toh*

toast
pane tostato
PA-neh toh-STA-toh

coffee with hot milk
caffelatte
kahf-feh-LAHT-teh

black coffee
caffè nero
kahf-FEH NEH-ro

. . . with milk
. . . con latte
. . . *kohn LAHT-teh*

. . . with sugar
. . . con zucchero
. . . *kohn DZOOK-keh-ro*

chocolate
cioccolata
chohk-ko-LA-ta

tea
tè
teh

. . . with lemon
. . . con limone
. . . *kohn lee-MO-neh*

a continental breakfast (coffee, rolls, butter, marmalade)
un caffè completo
oon kahf-FEH kohm-PLEH-toh

lunch
colazione
ko-lahts-YO-neh

dinner
pranzo
PRAHNT-so

Do you know a good restaurant?
Conosce un buon ristorante?
ko-NO-sheh oon bwohn ree-sto-RAHN-teh?

A table for three.
Una tavola per tre.
OO-na TA-vo-la pair treh.

This way, please.
Da questa parte, prego.
*da KWESS-ta PAR-teh,
PREH-go.*

The menu, please.
Il menù, prego.
eel meh-NOO, PREH-go.

What's good?
Cosa c'è di buono?
KO-za cheh dee BWO-no?

What do you recommend?
Cosa mi consiglia?
KO-za mee kohn-SEEL-ya?

What is this?
Cos'è questo?
ko-ZEH KWESS-toh?

Good.
Bene
BEH-neh.

I'll try it.
Lo proverò.
lo pro-veh-RO.

Give me this.
Mi dia questo.
*mee DEE-ya
KWESS-toh.*

First a cocktail.
Prima un aperitivo.
*PREE-ma oon ah-peh-ree-
TEE-vo.*

And then some antipasto.
E poi un po' d'antipasto.
*eh poy oon po dahn-tee-
PAHS-toh.*

soup
minestra
mee-NEHS-tra

fish
pesce
PEH-sheh

oysters
ostriche
OH-stree-keh

shrimps
scampi
SKAHM-pee

clams
vongole
VOHN-go-leh

lobster
aragosta
ah-ra-GO-sta

roasted
arrosto
ahr-RO-sto

broiled
alla griglia
AHL-la GREEL-ya

fried
fritto
FREET-toh

boiled
bollito
bohl-LEE-toh

chicken
pollo
POHL-lo

duck
anitra
AH-nee-tra

goose
oca
OH-ka

roast pork
arrosto de maiale
*ahr-RO-sto dee
ma-YA-leh*

pork chops
braciole di maiale
*bra-CHO-leh dee
ma-YA-leh*

veal chops
braciole de vitello
*bra-CHO-leh dee
vee-TEL-lo*

lamb chops
braciole d'agnello
bra-CHO-leh dahn-YEL-lo

roast lamb
arrosto di agnello
ahr-RO-sto dee ahn-YEL-lo

beef
manzo
MAHNT-so

meatballs
polpette
pohl-PET-teh

steak
bistecca
bee-STEK-ka

well done
ben cotta
ben KOHT-ta

medium
poco cotta
PO-ko KOHT-ta

rare
al sangue
ahl SAHN-gweh

bread
pane
PA-neh

butter
burro
BOOR-ro

with
con
kohn

without
senza
SENT-za

noodles
tagliatelle
tahl-ya-TEL-leh

rice
riso
REE-zo

vegetables
legumi
leh-GOO-mee

potatoes	**green beans**	**peas**
patate	fagiolini	piselli
pa-TA-teh	*fa-jo-LEE-nee*	*pee-ZEL-lee*

carrots	**spinach**	**tomatoes**
carote	spinaci	pomodori
ka-RO-teh	*spee-NA-chee*	*po-mo-DOH-ree*

cabbage	**onions**	**mushrooms**	**asparagus**
cavolo	cipolle	funghi	asparagi
KA-vo-lo	*chee-POHL-leh*	*FOON-ghee*	*ahs-PA-ra-jee*

lettuce	**salad**	**oil**	**vinegar**
lattuga	insalata	olio	aceto
laht-TOO-ga	*een-sa-LA-ta*	*OHL-yo*	*ah-CHEH-toh*

salt	**pepper**	**mustard**	**garlic**
sale	pepe	senape	aglio
SA-leh	*PEH-peh*	*SEH-na-peh*	*AHL-yo*

What wine do you recommend?
Quale vino mi consiglia?
KWA-leh VEE-no mee kohn-SEEL-ya?

white wine	**red wine**
vino bianco	vino rosso
VEE-no B'YAHN-ko	*VEE-no ROHS-so*

beer	**champagne**	**To your health!**
birra	sciampagna	Alla sua salute!
BEER-ra	*shahm-PAHN-ya*	*AHL-la SOO-ah sa-LOO-teh!*

fruit	**grapes**	**peaches**	**apples**
frutta	uva	pesche	mele
FROOT-ta	*OO-va*	*PEH-sheh*	*MEH-leh*

pears	bananas	strawberries	oranges
pere	banane	fragole	arance
PEH-reh	*ba-NA-neh*	*FRA-go-leh*	*ah-RAHN-cheh*

a dessert	pastry	cake
un dolce	paste	torta
oon DOHL-cheh	*PAHS-teh*	*TOHR-ta*

ice cream	cheese	expresso
gelato	formaggio	espresso
jeh-LA-toh	*for-MAHD-jo*	*ess-PRESS-so*

More, please.
Ancora, prego.
ahn-KO-ra, PREH-go.

That's enough, thank you.
Basta così, grazie.
BA-sta ko-ZEE, GRAHTS-yeh.

waiter	waitress
cameriere	cameriera
ka-mair-YEH-reh	*ka-mair-YEH-ra*

The check, please.
Il conto, prego.
eel KOHN-toh, PREH-go.

Is the service included?
Il servizio è compreso?
eel sair-VEETS-yo eh kohm-PREH-zo?

The bill is incorrect.
Il conto non è giusto.
eel KOHN-toh nohn eh JOOS-toh.

What do you think?	Isn't it so?
Che ne dice?	Non è vero?
keh neh DEE-cheh?	*nohn eh VEH-ro?*

Oh, no, sir, look here.
Ah, no, signore, guardi.
ah no, seen-YO-reh, GWAHR-dee.

Oh, now I understand.
Ah, adesso capisco.
ah, ah-DESS-so ka-PEES-ko.

You are right.
Ha ragione Lei.
ah ra-JO-neh lay.

It's all right.
Va bene.
va BEH-neh.

Thank you, sir.
Grazie, signore.
GRAHTS-yeh, seen-YO-reh.

Come again soon!
Torni presto!
TOR-nee PRESS-toh!

POINT TO THE ANSWER

When you are at a restaurant and you wish to make sure that you understand the menu, show the following section to the waiter so that he or she can select the answer. The sentence in Italian after the arrow asks him or her to point to the answer.

 La prego di mostrare qui sotto la Sua risposta alla mia domanda. Molte grazie!

Questa è la nostra specialità.
This is our speciality.

È pronto.
It's ready.

Non è pronto.
It's not ready.

Ci vogliono _____ minuti.
It takes _____ minutes.

Oggi non ne abbiamo.   **Soso il sabato.**
We don't have it today.   Only on Saturday.

pollo	**vitello**	**manzo**	**maiale**	**agnello**	**salsice**	**prosciutto**
chicken	veal	beef	pork	lamb	sausage	ham

coniglio	**frutti di mare**	**pesce**	**polipo**	**pasta**
rabbit	sea food	fish	squid	spaghetti, noodles, etc.

. . . con una salsa speciale   **. . . con spaghetti**
. . . with a special sauce   . . . with spaghetti

. . . con legumi
. . . with vegetables

9. Food Specialties of Italy

These expressions and names of dishes will be useful in restaurants or private homes where you may be invited. These dishes commonly appear on most Italian menus and are so much a part of Italian dining tradition that you should recognize them and know how to pronounce them as well as to enjoy them! We have written the Italian first, since that is how you will see it on the menus.

What is today's special?
Qual'è la specialità del giorno?
kwah-LEH la speh-cha-lee-TA del JOR-no?

Is it ready?
È pronto?
eh PROHN-toh?

How long will it take?
Quanto ci vorrà?
KWAHN-toh chee vor-RA?

Antipasto
ahn-tee-PA-sto
melon, ham, figs, olives, artichokes, salami

Minestrone
mee-neh-STRO-neh
vegetable soup

Timballo di riso
teem-BAHL-lo dee REE-zo
rice casserole

Cannelloni
kahn-nel-LO-nee
cheese rolled in pasta

Fettuccine al burro
feht-toot-CHEE-neh ahl BOOR-ro
noodles with butter and cheese

Risotto alla Milanese
ree-ZOHT-toh AHL-la mee-la-NEH-zeh
rice and saffron

Gnocchi alla Romana
N'YOHK-kee AHL-la ro-MA-na
dumplings baked with butter and cheese

Tagliatelle alla Bolognese
tahl-ya-TEL-leh AHL-la bo-lohn-YEH-zeh
noodles with meat sauce

Spaghetti alla carbonara
spa-GHET-tee AHL-la kar-
bo-NA-ra
spaghetti with egg sauce

Pasticcio di lasagne
pa-STEET-cho dee la-
SAHN-yeh
lasagna, cheese, meat

Cotolette alla Milanese
ko-toh-LET-teh AHL-la mee-la-NEH-zeh
veal, breaded and baked

Osso Buco
OHS-so BOO-ko
veal knuckles simmered with spices

Fegato alla Veneziana
FEH-ga-toh AHL-la veh-nehts-YA-na
liver with onions

Saltimbocca alla Romana
sahl-teem-BOHK-ka AHL-la ro-MA-na
veal with sage, ham, cheese, and wine

Pollo alla cacciatore
POHL-lo AHL-la kaht-cha-TOH-reh
braised chicken with black olive and anchovy sauce

Fritto Misto
FREET-toh MEES-toh
mixed seafood fried in batter

Scaloppine alla Marsala
ska-lohp-PEE-neh AHL-la mar-SA-la
veal with wine sauce

Costata alla Fiorentina
ko-STA-ta AHL-la fyo-ren-TEE-na
ribs of beef cooked over a wood fire

Cheeses:

Bel Paese
bel pa-EH-zeh

Gorgonzola
gor-gohnd-ZO-la

Stracchino
strahk-KEE-no

Provolone
pro-vo-LO-neh

Desserts:

Torta Mille Foglie
Tor-ta MEEL-leh FOHL-yeh
pastry with cream filling

Zabaglione
dza-bahl-YO-neh
whipped eggs with brandy and sugar

Cappuccino
kahp-poot-CHEE-no
coffee with whipped cream topping

Do you like it?
Le piace?
leh P'YA-cheh?

It's the best!
È ottimo!
eh OHT-tee-mo!

It's excellent!
È eccellente!
eh et-chel-LEN-teh!

It's my favorite dish!
È il mio piatto preferito!
eh eel MEE-yo P'YAHT-toh preh-feh-REE-toh!

Thank you for a wonderful dinner.
Grazie per la buonissima cena.
GRAHTS-yeh pair la bwo-NEES-see-ma CHEH-na.

It's nothing. (You are welcome.)
Di niente.
dee N'YEN-teh.

I'm happy that you enjoyed it.
Sono contento che Le sia piaciuta.
SO-no kohn-TEN-toh keh leh SEE-ya p'ya-CHOO-ta.

10. Transportation

Getting around by public transportation is enjoyable, not only for the new and interesting things you see but also because of the opportunities you have for practicing Italian. To make your travels easier use short phrases when speaking to drivers or others when you ask directions. And don't forget **prego** and **grazie**.

Bus

Bus.
Autobus.
OW-toh-booss.

Where is the bus stop?
Dov'è la fermata dell'autobus?
doh-VEH la fair-MA-ta del-L'OW-toh-booss?

Do you go to Piazza Garibaldi?
Va a Piazza Garibaldi?
va ah P'YAHT-tsa ga-ree-BAHL-dee?

No. Take number nine.
No. Prenda il numero nove.
no. PREN-da eel NOO-meh-ro NO-veh.

How much is the fare?
Quanto costa?
KWAHN-toh KO-sta?

Where do you want to go?
Dove vuole andare?
DOH-veh VWO-leh ahn-DA-reh?

To the cathedral.
Al duomo.
ahl DWO-mo.

Is it far?
È lontano?
eh lohn-TA-no?

No. It's near.
No. È vicino.
no. eh vee-CHEE-no.

Please tell me where to get off.
Per favore, me dica dove devo scendere.
pair fa-VO-reh, me DEE-ka DOH-veh DEH-vo SHEN-deh-reh.

Do I get off here?
Scendo qui?
SHEN-doh kwee?

POINT TO THE ANSWER

To make sure that you understand the answer to a question, show the following section to the Italian person you are talking to so that he or she can select the answer. The sentence in Italian after the arrow asks him or her to point to the answer to your question.

 La prego di mostrare qui sotto la Sua risposta alla mia domanda. Molte grazie!

Laggiù.
Over there.

Da quella parte.
That way.

All'angolo.
On the corner.

Dall'altra parte della strada.
On the other side of the street.

Diritto.
Straight ahead.

A destra.
To the right.

A sinistra.
To the left.

Non so.
I don't know.

Taxi

Taxi!
Tassì!
tahs-SEE!

Are you free?
È libero?
eh LEE-beh-ro?

Where to?
Dove?
DOH-veh?

To this address.
A questo indirizzo.
ah KWESS-toh een-dee-REET-tso.

Do you know where it is?
Sa dov'è?
sa doh-VEH?

I am in a hurry.
Ho fretta.
oh FRET-ta.

Go fast.
Vada in fretta.
VA-da een FRET-ta.

Slow down.
Vāda piano.
VA-da P'YA-no.

Stop here.
Si fermi qui.
see FAIR-mee kwee.

At the corner.
All'angolo.
ahl-LAHN-go-lo.

Wait for me.
Mi aspetti.
mee ah-SPET-tee.

Can one park here?
Si può parcheggiare qui?
see pwo par-keh-JA-reh k'wee?

I'll be back soon.
Torno subito.
TOR-no SOO-bee-toh.

In five minutes.
Tra cinque minuti.
tra CHEEN-kweh mee-NOO-tee.

More or less.
Più o meno.
p'yoo oh MEH-no.

How much is it per hour?
Quanto costa all'ora?
KWAHN-toh KO-sta ahl-LO-ra?

. . . per kilometer?
. . . all chilometro?
. . . ahl kee-LO-meh-tro?

Call for me tomorrow.
Mi venga a prendere domani.
mee VEN-ga ah PREN-deh-reh doh-MA-nee.

In the morning.
La mattina.
la maht-TEE-na.

In the afternoon.
Il pomeriggio.
eel po-meh-REED-jo.

At three o'clock sharp.
Alle tre in punto.
AHL-leh treh een POON-toh.

At the Hotel National.
All'Albergo Nazionale.
ahl-lahl-BAIR-go nahts-yo-NA-leh.

A proposito: Tip 10% or 15% of the meter. After midnight there is a surcharge.

POINT TO THE ANSWER

Show the following Italian sentence to your taxi driver so he or she can point to the appropriate answer below.

 Per favore indichi la risposta alla mia domanda su questa pagina. Grazie.

L'aspetto qui.
I will wait for you here.

Non posso aspettare.
I cannot wait.

Tornerò a prenderla.
I'll be back to pick you up.

Il bagaglio è extra.
The baggage is extra.

Non basta.
It is not enough.

Adesso va bene.
Now it's okay.

Trains and Subway

The subway.
La metropolitana.
la meh-tro-po-lee-TA-na.

Is there a subway in this city?
C'è una metropolitana in questa città?
cheh OO-na meh-tro-po-lee-TA-na een KWESS-ta cheet-TA?

Where is the subway?
Dov'è la metropolitana?
doh-VEH la meh-tro-po-lee-TA-na?

The train.
Il treno.
eel TREH-no.

Where is the station?
Dov'è la stazione?
doh-VEH la stahts-YO-neh?

Where can I buy the tickets?
Dove posso comprare i biglietti?
DOH-veh POHS-so kohm-PRA-reh ee beel-YET-tee?

One ticket for Venice.
Un biglietto per Venezia.
oon beel-YET-toh pair veh-NEHTS-ya.

Round trip.
Andata e ritorno.
ahn-DA-ta eh ree-TOR-no.

One way only.
Andata solo.
ahn-DA-ta SO-lo.

First class.
Prima classe.
PREE-ma KLAHS-seh.

Second class
Seconda classe.
seh-KOHN-da KLAHS-seh.

A timetable.
Un orario.
oon oh-RAR-yo.

Where is the train for Milan?
Dov'è il treno per Milano?
doh-VEH eel TREH-no pair mee-LA-no?

When do we leave?
A che ora si parte?
ah keh OH-ra see PAR-teh?

Is this seat taken?
Questo posto è occupato?
KWESS-toh PO-sto eh ohk-koo-PA-toh?

With your permission, madam.
Permesso, signora.
pair-MES-so, seen-YO-ra.

Of course, sir.
Certo, signore.
CHAIR-toh, seen-YO-reh.

At what time do we arrive in Florence?
A che ora arriviamo a Firenze?
ah keh OH-ra ahr-reev-YA-mo ah fee-RENT-seh?

Does the train stop in Bologna?
Si ferma il treno a Bologna?
see FAIR-ma eel TREH-no ah bo-LOHN-ya?

How long are we stopping here?
Quanto ci fermiamo qui?
KWAHN-toh chee fairm-YA-mo kwee?

Where is the dining car?
Dov'è il vagone ristorante?
doh-VEH eel va-GO-neh ree-sto-RAHN-teh?

I can't find my ticket.
Non trovo il mio biglietto.
nohn TRO-vo eel MEE-yo beel-YET-toh.

Wait!
Aspetti!
ah-SPET-tee!

Here it is.
Eccolo.
EK-ko-lo.

Prepare my berth, please.
Mi prepari la cuccetta, per favore.
mee preh-PA-ree la koot-CHET-ta, pair fa-VO-reh.

Can you help me?
Mi può aiutare?
mee pwo ah-yoo-TA-reh?

I took the wrong train.
Ho sbagliato treno.
oh zbahl-YA-toh TREH-no.

I wish to go to Naples.
Vorrei andare a Napoli.
vohr-RAY ahn-DA-reh ah NA-po-lee.

POINT TO THE ANSWER

The answers below will help you in your travels by rail in Italy. Show the first sentence to the conductor or station guard so he can select the answer. The sentence in Italian next to the arrow asks him to point to the answer.

 Per favore indichi la risposta alla mia domanda su questa pagina. Grazie.

Marciapiede numero _____
Track number _____

Da quella parte. **Sotto.** **Sopra.**
That way. Downstairs. Upstairs.

Partirà fra _____ minuti.
It leaves in _____ minutes.

Questo non è il suo treno.
This is not your train.

Non va a _____.
It doesn't go to _____.

Deve cambiare a _____.
You must change at _____.

Arriveremo alle _____.
We will arrive at _____ o'clock.

Ship

What time does the ship sail?
A che ora parte la nave?
ah keh OH-ra PAR-teh la NA-veh?

From which pier?
Da quale banchina?
da KWA-leh bahn-KEE-na?

Where is my cabin?
Dov'è la mia cabina?
doh-VEH la MEE-ya ka-BEE-na?

Where is my luggage?
Dove sono le mie valigie?
DOH-veh SO-no leh MEE-yeh va-LEE-jeh?

Please take my luggage to my cabin.
Prego porti le mie valigie in cabina.
PREH-go POR-tee leh MEE-yeh va-LEE-jeh een ka-BEE-na.

Where is . . .	**. . . the purser?**	**. . . the bar?**
Dov'è . . .	. . . il commisario?	. . . il bar?
doh-VEH . . .	*. . . eel ko-mees-SAR-yo?*	*. . . eel bar?*

. . . the dining salon?	**. . . the movie?**
. . . la sala da pranzo?	. . . il cinema?
. . . la SA-la da PRAHNT-so?	*. . . eel CHEE-neh-ma?*

. . . the card room?	**. . . the swimming pool?**
. . . la sala da gioco?	. . . la piscina?
. . . la SA-la da JO-ko?	*. . . la pee-SHEE-na?*

first class	**tourist class**
prima classe	classe turistica
PREE-ma KLAHS-seh	*KLAHS-seh too-REES-tee-ka*

a yacht
un yacht
oon yoht

a motorboat
una barca a motore
*OO-na BAR-ka ah mo-TOH-
    reh*

a sailboat
una barca va vela
OO-na BAR-ka ah VEH-la

a ferry
un traghetto
oon tra-GHET-toh

a gondola
una gondola
OO-na GOHN-doh-la

Gondolier, sing us a song.
Gondoliere, ci canti una canzone.
*gohn-dohl-YEH-reh, chee KAHN-tee OO-na kahnt-SO-
    neh.*

Do you know "Torna a Sorrento"?*
Conosce Torna a Sorrento?
co-NO-sheh TOR-na ah sor-REN-toh?

---

*"Come Back to Sorrento"

11. Trips by Car

Car Rental

Where can one rent a car?
Dove si può noleggiare una macchina?
DOH-veh see pwo no-led-JA-reh OO-na MAHK-kee-na?

. . . a motorcycle?
. . . una motocicletta?
. . . OO-na mo-toh-chee-KLET-ta?

. . . a bicycle?
. . . una bicicletta?
. . . OO-na bee-chee-KLET-ta?

I want to rent a car.
Desidero noleggiare una macchina.
deh-ZEE-deh-ro no-led-JA-reh OO-na MAHK-kee-na.

How much per day?
Quanto costa al giorno?
KWAHN-toh KO-sta ahl JOR-no?

How much per kilometer?
Quanto al chilometro?
KWAHN-toh ahl kee-LO-meh-tro?

Is the gasoline included?
La benzina è compresa?
la bend-ZEE-na eh kom-PREH-za?

Is the transmission automatic?
Ha il cambio automatico?
ah eel KAHMB-yo ow-toh-MA-tee-ko?

would like to try it out.
Vorrei provarla.
vor-RAY pro-VAR-la.

A proposito: Distances are reckoned in kilometers, approximately ⅝ of a mile.

53

Gas Station

Where can I buy gasoline?
Dove posso comprare della benzina?
DOH-veh POHS-so kohm-PRA-reh DEL-la bend-ZEE-na?

How much per liter?
Quanto al litro?
KWAHN-toh ahl LEE-tro?

Thirty liters, please.
Trenta litri, per piacere.
TREHN-ta LEE-tree, pair p'ya-CHEH-reh.

Fill it up.
Faccia il pieno.
FAHT-cha eel p'YEH-no.

Please . . .
Per favore . . .
pair fa-VO-reh . . .

Put air in the tires.
Pompi le gomme.
POHM-pee leh GOHM-meh.

Check the water.
Controlli l'acqua.
kohn-TROHL-lee LAHK-kwa.

. . . the battery.
. . . la batteria.
. . . la baht-teh-REE-ya.

. . . the oil.
. . . l'olio.
. . . LOHL-yo.

. . . the spark plugs.
. . . le candele.
. . . leh kahn-DEH-leh.

. . . the carburetor.
. . . il carburatore.
. . . eel kar-boo-ra-TOH-reh.

. . . the brakes.
. . . i freni.
. . . ee FREH-nee.

Change the oil.
Cambi l'olio.
KAHM-bee LOHL-yo.

Grease the motor.
Ingrassi il motore.
een-GRAHS-see eel mo-TOH-reh.

Change this tire.
Cambi questa gomma.
KAHM-bee KWESS-ta GOHM-ma.

Wash the car.
Lavi la macchina.
LA-vee la MAHK-kee-na.

A road map, please.
Una mappa stradale, prego.
OO-na MAHP-pa strah-DA-leh, PREH-go.

A proposito: Gas is sold by the liter (1.05 quarts). In other words, four liters is about one gallon.

Asking Directions

Where does this road go?
Dove va questa strada?
DOH-veh va KWESS-ta STRA-da?

Is this the way to Turin?
È questa la strada per Torino?
eh KWESS-ta la STRA-da pair toh-REE-no?

Is the road good?
È una buona strada?
eh OO-na BWO-na STRA-da?

Which is the road for Verona?
Qual'è la strada per Verona?
kwa-LEH la STRA-da pair veh-RO-na?

It's that way.
Da quella parte.
da KWEL-la PAR-teh.

Is the next town far?
È lontana la prossimo città?
eh lohn-TA-na la PROHS-see-ma cheet-TA?

Do you know if there is a good restaurant there?
Sa se c'è un buon ristorante lì?
Sa seh cheh oon bwohn ree-sto-RAHN-teh lee?

. . . a good hotel?
. . . un buon albergo?
. . . *oon bwohn ahl-BEHR-go?*

What is it called?
Come si chiama?
Co-meh see k'ya-ma?

Is it far?
È lontano?
eh lohn-TA-no?

POINT TO THE ANSWER

To make sure that you understand the answer to your questions about driving directions, show the following section to the person whom you are asking. The sentence in Italian next to the arrow asks him or her to point to the answer.

 La prego di mostrare qui sotto la Sua risposta alla mia domanda. Molte grazie!

Si chiama . . .
It's called . . .

Segua questa strada.
Follow this road.

Circa cinquanta kilometri.
About fifty kilometers.

Lei è in questo punto su questa carta.
You are at this point on this map.

Il prossimo paese si chiama _____
The next village is called _____

Volti a destra all'uscita del paese.
Turn right as you leave the village.

Volti a sinistra al semaforo.
Turn right at the traffic light.

Allora vada diritto.
Then go straight.

Quando arriva al ponte . . .
When you come to the bridge . . .

attraversi, e volti a sinistra.
cross it and turn left.

Continui fino all'autostrada.
Continue on to the expressway.

Ma attenzione!   **C'è un limite di velocità.**
But be careful!   There's a speed limit.

Emergencies and Repairs

Your license!   **Here it is, officer!**
La patente!   Eccola, Signor Agente!
la pa-TEN-teh!   *EK-ko-la, seen-YOR ah-*
                                      JEN-teh!

And the registration.
E i documenti della macchina.
eh ee doh-koo-MEHN-tee DEL-la MAHK-kee-na.

It wasn't my fault.   **The truck skidded.**
Non è stata colpa mia.   Il camion ha slittato.
nohn eh STA-ta KOHL-pa   *eel KAHM-yohn ah zleet-TA-*
  MEE-ya.   *toh.*

This imbecile crashed into me.
Quest'imbecille mi è venuto contro.
KWEST-eem-beh-CHEEL-leh mee eh veh-NOO-toh
  KOHN-tro.

A proposito: As Italians drive with considerable dash and challenge, **imbecille, idiota, brutto,** and **cretino** (dumb fool) are frequent and rather mild expletives. However, control and good humor, plus a diplomatic use of Italian, will make driving safe and enjoyable.

I need help.
Ho bisogno d'aiuto.
oh bee-ZOHN-yo da-YOO-toh.

Could you help me?
Mi può aiutare?
mee pwo ah-yoo-TA-reh?

My car has broken down.
La mia macchina non funziona.
la MEE-ya MAHK-kee-na nohn foonts-YO-na.

It's stuck.
Non va avanti.
nohn va ah-VAHN-tee.

I have a flat tire.
Ho una gomma a terra.
oh OO-na GOHM-ma ah TAIR-ra.

Can you lend me a jack?
Mi può imprestare un cricco?
mee pwo eem-press-TA-reh oon KREEK-ko?

Can you push me?
Mi può spingere?
mee pwo-SPEEN-jeh-reh?

Thank you very much.
Grazie tante.
GRAHTS-yeh TAHN-teh.

You are very kind.
Lei è molto gentile.
lay eh MOHL-toh jen-TEE-leh.

I want to see the mechanic.
Voglio vedere il meccanico.
VOHL-yo veh-DEH-reh eel mek-KA-nee-ko.

He doesn't work on weekends.
Non lavora il week-end.
nohn la-VO-ra eel week-end.

What's the matter?
Che cos'è?
keh ko-ZEH?

The car doesn't run well.
La macchina non va bene.
la MAHK-kee-na nohn va BEH-neh.

There is a funny noise in the motor.
C'è un rumore strano nel motore.
cheh oon roo-MO-reh STRA-no nel mo-TOH-reh.

It's difficult to start.
È difficile metterla in moto.
eh dee-FEE-chee-leh MET-tair-la een MO-toh.

Can you fix it?
Può aggiustarla?
pwo ahd-joos-TAR-la?

What will it cost?
Quanto costerà?
KWAHN-toh ko-steh-RA?

How long will it take?
Quanto tempo ci vorrà?
KWAHN-toh TEM-po chee vor-RA?

I'm in a hurry.
Ho fretta.
oh FRET-ta.

When will it be ready?
Quando sarà pronta?
KWAHN-doh sa-RA PROHN-ta?

POINT TO THE ANSWER

To make sure you understand the mechanic, show him the Italian sentence next to the arrow and let him point to the answer.

 Per favore indichi la risposta alla mia domanda su questa pagina. Grazie.

Fra una (due) (tre) ore.
In one (two) (three) hours.

Oggi non è possibile.
Today isn't possible.

Forse domani.
Perhaps tomorrow.

Dopo domani.
The day after tomorrow.

La macchina sarà pronta fra _____ giorni.
The car will be ready in _____ days.

Non abbiamo il pezzo di ricambio.
We don't have the spare part.

Possiamo ripararla provvisoriamente.
We can repair it temporarily.

Costerà _____ lire.
It will cost _____ lire.

Ha bisogno anche di una gomma nova.
You also need a new tire.

International Road Signs

Danger

Caution

Sharp turn

Crossroads

Right curve

Left curve

Guarded RR crossing

Unguarded RR crossing

Main road ahead

Bumps

One way

Do not enter

No parking

Parking

As you drive in Italy, you would see or hear the following instructions.

Here the Italian is given first, since this is how you will hear or see the instructions:

TENERE LA DESTRA
teh-NEH-reh la DESS-tra
Keep to the right

SENSO UNICO
SEN-so OO-nee-ko
One way

VELOCITÀ MASSIMA
veh-lo-chee-TA MAHS-see-ma
Maximum speed

RALLENTARE
rahl-len-TA-reh
Slow down

LAVORI IN CORSO
la-VO-ree een KOR-so
Work in progress

RITORNO SUBITO
ree-TOR-no SOO-bee-toh
Sharp turn

PASSAGIO DI LEVELLO
pa-SA-jo dee leh-VEL-lo
Railroad crossing

CURVA A DESTRA
KOOR-va ah DESS-tra
Right curve

ENTRATA PRIOBITA
en-TRA-ta pro-ee-BEE-ta
Do not enter

DEVIAZIONE
dev-yahts-YO-neh
Detour

INCROCIO
een-KRO-cho
Crossroads

CHILOMETRI
kee-LO-meh-tree
kilometers

NON PARCHEGGIARE
nohn par-kay-JAR-reh
No parking

PERICULO
peh-REE-koo-lo
Danger

ATTENZIONE
aht-tents-YO-neh
Caution

VIA PRINCIPALE AVANTI
VEE-ah preen-chee-PA-leh ah-VAHN-tee
Main road ahead

CURVA A SINISTRA
KOOR-va ah see-NEESS-tra
Left curve

STAZIONE DI BENZINA
stahts-YO-neh dee bend-ZEE-na
Gas station

12. Sight-seeing and Photography

We have combined these two important sections, since you will want to take pictures of what you are seeing. If you are taking pictures indoors, be sure to ask the custodian, "Is it permitted?"—È permesso?

I need a guide.
Ho bisogno di una guida.
oh bee-ZOHN-yo dee OO-na GWEE-da.

Are you a guide?
Lei è una guida?
lay eh OO-na GWEE-da?

Do you speak English?
Parla inglese?
PAR-la een-GLEH-zeh?

It doesn't matter.
Non importa.
nohn eem-POR-ta.

I speak a little Italian.
Parlo un po' d'italiano.
PAR-lo oon po dee-tahl-YA-no.

Do you have a car?
Ha una macchina?
ah OO-na MAHK-kee-na?

How much do you charge per hour?
Quanto richiede all'ora?
KWAHN-toh reek-YEH-deh ahl-LO-ra?

How much per day?
Quanto al giorno?
KWAHN-toh ahl JOR-no?

For two people?
Per due persone?
pair DOO-weh pair-SO-neh?

A group of four?
Un gruppo di quattro?
oon GROOP-po dee KWAHT-tro?

We would like to see the old part of the city.
Desideriamo vedere la parte vecchia della città.
deh-zee-dair-YA-mo veh-DEH-reh la PAR-teh VEHK-k'ya DEL-la cheet-TA.

Where is the Piazza Garibaldi?
Dov'è Piazza Garibaldi?
doh-VEH P'YAHT-tsa ga-ree-BAHL-dee?

We want to go . . .
Vogliamo andare . . .
VOHL-ya-mo ahn-DA-reh . . .

. . . to the Pitti Palace.
. . . a Palazzo Pitti.
. . . ah pa-LAHT-tso PEET-tee.

. . . to the Vatican.
. . . al Vaticano.
. . . ahl va-tee-KA-no.

. . . to the Piazza Navona.
. . . a Piazza Navona.
. . . ah P'YAHT-tsa na-VO-na

. . . to the gardens.
. . . ai giardini.
. . . I jar-DEE-nee.

. . . to the zoo.
. . . allo zoo.
. . . AHL-lo DZO-oh.

. . . to the market.
. . . al mercato.
. . . ahl mair-KA-toh.

. . . to the ruins.
. . . alle rovine.
. . . AHL-leh ro-VEE-neh.

. . . to the Cathedral.
. . . al Duomo.
. . . ahl DWO-mo.

. . . to the Roman Forum.
. . . al Foro Romano.
. . . ahl FO-ro ro-MA-no.

. . . to the Colosseum.
. . . al Colosseo.
. . . ahl ko-lohs-SEH-yo.

. . . to the Baths of Caracalla.
. . . alle Terme di Caracalla.
. . . AHL-leh TAIR-meh dee ka-ra-KAHL-la.

. . . to the Old Bridge.
. . . al Ponte Vecchio.
. . . ahl POHN-teh VEHK-k'yo.

. . . to the Tower of Pisa.
. . . alla Torre di Pisa.
. . . AHL-la TOR-reh dee PEE-za.

How beautiful!
Che bello!
keh BEL-lo!

Very interesting!
Molto interessante!
*MOHL-toh een-teh-ress-
SAHN-teh!*

From what period is this?
Di che epoca è questo?
dee keh EH-po-ka eh KWESS-toh?

Do you know a good cabaret?
Conosce un buon locale notturno?
ko-NO-sheh oon bwohn lo-KA-leh not-TOOR-no?

Let's go.
Andiamo.
ahnd-YA-mo.

You are a very good guide.
Lei è un' ottima guida.
*lay eh oon OHT-tee-ma
GWEE-da.*

Come again tomorrow.
Torni domani.
TOR-nee doh-MA-nee.

At nine o'clock sharp.
Alle nove in punto.
*AHL-leh NO-veh een
POON-toh.*

And, if you don't have a guide:

May one enter?
Si può entrare?
see pwo en-TRA-reh?

It is open.
È aperto.
eh ah-PAIR-toh.

It is closed.
È chiuso.
eh K'YOO-zo.

It opens at two o'clock.
Si apre alle due.
*see AH-preh AHL-leh DOO-
weh.*

What are the visiting hours?
Qual'è l'orario delle visite?
kwa-LEH lo-RAR-yo DEL-leh VEE-zee-teh?

It is closed for repairs.
È chiuso per restauri.
eh K'YOO-zo pair rest-OW-ree.

Can one take photos?
È permesso fare fotografie?
eh pair-MESS-so FA-reh fo-toh-gra-FEE-yeh?

It is permitted.
È permesso.
eh pair-MESS-so.

It is forbidden.
È vietato.
eh v'yeh-TA-toh.

Leave your packages in the checkroom.
Lasci i pacchi al guardaroba.
LA-shee ee PAHK-kee ahl gwar-da-RO-ba.

Leave your camera.
Lasci la macchina fotografica.
LA-shee la MAHK-kee-na fo-toh-GRA-fee-ka.

What is the admission?
Quanto costa l'entrata?
KWAHN-toh KO-sta len-TRA-ta?

Two hundred lire.
Duecento lire.
DOO-weh-CHEN-toh LEE-reh.

And, for children?
E per i bambini?
eh pair ee bahm-BEE-nee?

The admission is free.
L'entrata è gratis.
len-TRA-ta eh GRA-teess.

Ticket, please.
Biglietto, prego.
beel-YET-toh, PREH-go.

Follow me.
Mi segua.
mee SEH-gwa.

This way.
Da questa parte.
da KWESS-ta PAR-teh.

This castle ...
Questo castello ...
KWESS-toh ka-STEL-lo ...

This palace ...
Questo palazzo ...
KWESS-toh pa-LAHT-tso ...

This church . . .
Questa chiesa . . .
KWESS-ta K'YEH-za . . .

This monument . . .
Questo monumento . . .
KWESS-toh mo-noo-MEN-toh . . .

This street . . .
Questa strada . . .
KWESS-ta STRA-da . . .

This square . . .
Questa piazza . . .
KWESS-ta P'YAHT-tsa . . .

What is it?
Che cos'è?
keh ko-ZEH?

It's very interesting!
È molto interessante!
eh MOHL-toh een-teh-ress-SAHN-teh!

It's magnificent!
È magnifico!
eh mahn-YEE-fee-ko!

It's very old, isn't it?
È molto antico, vero?
eh MOHL-toh ahn-TEE-ko, VEH-ro?

This is for you.
Questo è per Lei.
KWESS-toh eh pair lay.

Some signs you may see in public places:

SIGNORI
seen-YO-ree
Gentlemen

SIGNORE
seen-YO-reh
Ladies

ENTRATA
en-TRA-ta
Entrance

USCITA
oo-SHEE-ta
Exit

APERTO
ah-PAIR-toh
Open

CHIUSO
K'YOO-zo
Closed

CALDO
KAHL-doh
Hot

FREDDO
FRED-doh
Cold

SPINGERE
SPEEN-jeh-reh
Push

TIRARE
tee-RA-reh
Pull

OGETTI PERDUTI
ohd-JET-tee pair-DOO-tee
Lost and found

ORARIO DELLE VISITE
oh-RAHR-yo DEL-leh VEE-zee-teh
Visiting hours

INFORMAZIONI
een-for-mahts-YO-nee
Information

GUARDAROBA
gwar-da-RO-ba
Checkroom

VIETATO FUMARE
v'yeh-TA-toh foo-MA-reh
No smoking

VIETATO ENTRARE
v'yeh-TA-toh en-TRA-reh
No admittance

A proposito: The word **vietato** in signs has the general connotation "No!" or "Don't do it!" So when you see it, don't walk on the grass, smoke, photograph, or whatever the case may be.

Photography

Where is a camera shop?
Dov'è un negozio d macchine fotografiche?
doh-VEH oon neh-GOHTS-yo dee MAHK-kee-neh fo-toh-GRA-fee-keh?

I would like some film.
Vorrei una pellicola.
vohr-RAY OO-na pel-LEE-ko-la.

. . . **movie film.**
. . . un film.
. . . *oon film.*

. . . in black and white.
. . . in bianco e nero.
. . . en B'YAHN-ko eh NEH-ro.

. . . in color.
. . . a colori.
. . . ah ko-LO-ree.

This is to be developed.
Questo è da sviluppare.
KWESS-toh eh da zvee-loop-PA-reh.

How much per print?
Quanto costa ogni fotografia?
KWAHN-toh KO-sta OHN-yee fo-toh-gra-FEE-ya?

Two of each.
Due di ognuna.
DOO-weh dee ohn-YOO-na.

An enlargement.
Un ingrandimento.
oon een-grahn-dee-MEN-toh.

About this size.
Circa di questa misura.
CHEER-ka dee KWESS-ta mee-ZOO-ra.

When will it be ready?
Quando sarà pronto?
KWAHN-doh sa-RA PROHN-toh?

Flashbulbs.
Flash.
flahsh.

For this camera.
Per questa macchina.
pair KWESS-ta MAHK-kee-na.

It's broken.
È rotta.
eh ROHT-ta.

Can you fix it?
Può aggiustarla?
pwo ad-joos-TAR-la?

May I take a photograph of you?
Le posso fare una fotografia?
leh POHS-so FA-ray OO-na fo-toh-gra-FEE-ya?

Stand here.
Resti qui.
RESS-tee kwee.

Don't move.
Non si muova.
nohn see MWO-va.

Smile.	**That's it.**
Sorrida.	Ecco fatto.
sohr-REE-da.	*EK-ko FAHT-toh.*

Will you please take one of me?
Sia gentile, mi faccia una foto?
SEE-ya jen-TEE-leh, mee FAHT-cha OO-na FO-toh?

In front of this.	**You are very kind.**
Qui davanti.	Lei è molto gentile.
kwee da-VAHN-tee.	*lay eh MOHL-toh jen-TEE-leh.*

May I send you a copy?
Le posso mandare una copia?
leh POHS-so mahn-DA-reh OO-na KOHP-ya?

Your name, please?
Il Suo nome, prego?
eel SOO-wo NO-meh, PREH-go?

Your address?
Il Suo indirizzo?
eel SOO-wo een-dee-REET-tso?

A proposito: Asking to take pictures of someone often leads to more general conversation. For this reason the following three sections will be especially interesting to you.

POINT TO THE ANSWER

To facilitate your dealings with an employee of the *negozio di macchine fotografichie*, point to the line in Italian below and await the answer.

 Per favore indichi la risposta alla mia domanda sulla prossima pagina. Grazie.

Ritorni domani.
Come back tomorrow.

Alle _____ ore.
At _____ o'clock.

Ritorni fra _____ giorni.
Come back in _____ days.

Possiamo ripararla.
We can repair it.

Non possiamo ripararla.
We cannot repair it.

Non ne abbiamo.
We haven't any.

13. Entertainment

This section will show you how to extend and accept invitations and to suggest things to do. It includes some typical conversations for theaters and nightclubs and some suitable words of appreciation when you are asked for dinner.

Things to Do

May I invite you . . .
Posso invitarLa . . .
*POHS-so een-vee-TAR-la
. . .*

. . . to lunch?
. . . a colazione?
. . . *ah ko-lahts-YO-neh?*

. . . to dinner?
. . . a pranzo?
. . . *ah PRAHNT-so?*

. . . for a drink?
. . . per un aperitivo?
. . . *pair oon ah-peh-ree-
TEE-vo?*

. . . to go for a drive?
. . . per un giro in macchina?
. . . *pair oon JEE-ro een
MAHK-kee-na?*

. . . to dance?
. . . a ballare?
. . . *ah bahl-LA-reh?*

. . . to play bridge?
. . . a giocare a bridge?
. . . *ah jo-KA-reh ah breej?*

. . . to the movies?
. . . al cinema?
. . . *ahl CHEE-neh-ma?*

. . . to the theater?
. . . a teatro?
. . . *ah teh-AH-tro?*

. . . to play golf
. . . a giocare a golf?
. . . *ah jo-KA-reh ah gohlf?*

. . . to play tennis?
. . . a giocare a tennis?
. . . *ah jo-KA-reh al tennis?*

Thank you very much.
Grazie infinite.
*GRAHTS-yeh een-fee-NEE-
teh.*

With pleasure.
Con piacere.
kohn p'ya-CHEH-reh.

I am sorry.
Mi dispiace.
Me dees-P'YA-cheh.

I cannot.
Non posso.
nohn POHS-so.

I am busy.
Sono occupato (m).
SO-no ohk-koo-PA-toh.
Sono occupata (f).
SO-no ohk-koo-PA-ta.

I am tired.
Sono stanco (m).
SO-no STAHN-ko.
Sono stanca (f).
SO-no STAHN-ka.

I am waiting for someone.
Sto aspettando qualcuno.
sto ah-spet-TAHN-doh kwahl-KOO-no.

I don't feel well.
Non mi sento bene.
nohn mee SEN-toh BEH-neh.

Maybe later.
Forse più tardi.
FOR-seh p'yoo TAR-dee.

Where are we going tomorrow?
Dove andiamo domani?
DOH-veh ahnd-YA-mo doh-MA-nee?

Let's go . . .
Andiamo . . .
ahnd-YA mo . . .

. . . around town.
. . . in giro per la città.
. . . een JEE-ro pair la cheet-TA.

. . . to the opera.
. . . all'opera.
. . . ahl-LO-peh-ra.

. . . to the art museum.
. . . al museo d'arte.
. . . ahl moo-ZEH-oh DAR-teh.

. . . to the palace.
. . . al palazzo.
. . . ahl pa-LAHT-tso.

. . . to the market.
. . . al mercato.
. . . ahl mair-KA-toh.

. . . to the center of town.
. . . al centro.
. . . ahl CHEN-tro.

. . . to the park.
. . . ai giardini
. . . I jar-DEE-nee.

. . . to the zoo.
. . . allo zoo.
. . . *AHL-lo DZO-oh.*

. . . to a fashion show.
. . . ad una mostra di moda.
. . . *ahd OO-na MO-stra dee MO-da.*

. . . to an art show.
. . . ad un'esposizione di quadri.
. . . *ahd oon-es-po-zeets-YO-neh dee KWAHD-ree.*

. . . for a ride in a gondola.
. . . a fare un giro in gondola.
. . . *ah FA-reh oon JEE-ro een GOHN-doh-la.*

. . . to the film festival.
. . . al festival del cinema.
. . . *ahl fes-tee-VAHL del CHEE-neh-ma.*

. . . to the movies.
. . . al cinema.
. . . *ahl CHEE-neh-ma.*

. . . to the meeting.
. . . alla riunione.
. . . *AHL-la ree-yoon-YO-neh.*

. . . to the beach.
. . . alla spiaggia.
. . . *AHL-la SP'YAHD-ja.*

. . . to the races.
. . . alle corse.
. . . *AHL-leh KOR-seh.*

to the soccer game.
. . . alla partita di calcio.
. . . *AHL-la par-TEE-ta dee KAHL-cho.*

Who's ahead?
Chi sta vincendo?
kee sta veen-CHEN-doh?

Theaters and Nightclubs

Let's go to the theater.
Andiamo a teatro.
ahnd-YA-mo ah teh-AH-tro.

Two seats, please.
Due posti, per piacere.
DOO-weh PO-stee, pair p'ya-CHEH-reh.

In the orchestra.
In platea.
een pla-TEH-ya.

In the balcony.
In galleria.
een gahl-leh-REE-ya.

Are they good seats?
Sono posti buoni?
SO-no PO-stee BWO-nee?

When does it start?
Quando comincia?
KWAHN-doh ko-MEEN-cha?

Who is playing the lead?
Chi ha la parte principale?
kee ah la PAR-teh preen-chee-PA-leh?

How beautiful she is!
Com'è bella!
ko-MEH BEL-la!

What do you think of it?
Che ne pensi?
keh neh PEN-see?

It's great.
È favoloso.
eh fa-vo-LO-zo.

I like it.
Mi piace.
mee P'YA-cheh.

It's very amusing.
È molto divertente.
eh MOHL-toh dee-vair-TEN-teh.

The second act is too long.
Il secondo atto è troppo lungo.
eel seh-KOHN-doh aht-toh eh TROHP-po LOON-go.

(Is it) over?
Finito?
fee-NEE-toh?

Did you like it?
Le è piaciuto?
leh eh p'ya-CHOO-toh?

Let's go to a nightclub.
Andiamo in un locale notturno.
ahnd-YA-mo een oon la-KA-leh noht-TOOR-no.

Is there a minimum charge?
C'è un prezzo minimo?
cheh oon PRET-zo MEE-nee-mo?

A table near the dance floor.
Un tavolo vicino alla pista da ballo.
oon TA-vo-lo vee-CHEE-no AHL-la PEE-sta da BAHL-lo.

Shall we dance?	**Shall we stay?**	**Let's go.**
Balliamo?	Restiamo?	Andiamo.
bahl-L'YA-mo?	*rest-YA-mo?*	*ahnd-YA-mo.*

A proposito: To express admiration for a performer in the arts or sports, one says *Bravo!* for a man and *Brava!* for a woman or, with even more enthusiasm, *Bravissimo!* and *Bravissima!*

An Invitation to Dinner

Can you come for dinner at our house, Monday at 8?
Può venire a pranzo da noi lunedì alle otto?
pwo veh-NEER-reh ah PRAHNT-so da noy loo-neh-DEE AHL-leh OHT-toh?

With pleasure.
Con piacere.
kohn p'ya-CHEH-reh.

If it isn't inconvenient for you.
Se non La disturba troppo.
seh nohn la-dees-TOOR-ba TROHP-po.

Sorry I'm late.
Scusi il ritardo.
SKOO-zee eel ree-TAR-doh.

The traffic was terrible!
C'era un traffico terribile!
CHEH-ra oon TRAHF-fee-ko tair-REE-bee-leh!

Very happy to see you.
Che piacere vederLa.
keh p'ya-CHEH-reh veh-DAIR-la.

Make yourself at home.
Si accomodi.
see ahk-KO-mo-dee.

What a beautiful house!
Che bella casa!
keh BEL-la KA-za!

Will you have something to drink?
Desidera qualcosa da bere?
deh-ZEE-deh-ra kwahl-KO-za da BEH-reh?

A cigarette?
Sigaretta?
see-ga RET-ta?

To your health!
Alla salute!
AHL-la sa-LOO-teh!

Dinner is served.
Il pranzo è servito.
eel PRAHNT-so eh sair-VEE-toh.

Will you sit here, please?
Vuole sedersi qui, per favore?
V'WO-leh seh-DAIR-see kwee, pair fa-VO-reh?

What a delicious meal!
Che pranzo squisito!
keh PRAHNT-so skwee-ZEE-toh!

Do have some more!
Si serva ancora!
see SAIR-va ahn-KO-ra!

We had a wonderful time.
Ci siamo divertiti moltissimo.
chee S'YA-mo dee-vair-TEE-tee mohl-TEES-see-mo.

I am sorry, but we must go.
Mi scusi ma dobbiamo andare.
mee-SKOO-zee ma dohb-B'YA-mo ahn-DA-reh.

We are taking the plane early tomorrow.
Domani prendiamo l'aereo di mattina presto.
doh-MA-nee prend-YA-mo la-ehr-yo dee maht-TEE-na PRESS-toh.

What a pity!
Che peccato!
keh pek-KA-toh!

We'll drive you back.
Vi riacompagniamo in macchina.
vee ree-yahk-kohm-pahn-YA-mo in MAHK-kee-na.

No, please don't bother.
No, per favore non si disturbi.
no, pair fa-VO-reh nohn see dees-TOOR-bee.

Many thanks for your hospitality.
Grazie infinite per la vostra ospitalità.
GRAHTS-yeh een-fee-NEE-teh pair la VO-stra oh-spee-ta-
   lee-TA.

You are welcome.
Prego
PREH-go.

It was a pleasure for us.
È stato un piacere per noi.
eh STA-toh oon p'ya-CHEH-reh pair noy.

Good-bye. Have a good trip!
Arrivederci. Buon viaggio!
ah-ree-va-DEHR-chee. bwohn V'YA-jo!

And come back to Italy soon.
E ritorni presto in Italia.
eh ree-TOR-nee PRESS-toh een ee-TAHL-ya.

14. Talking to People

Most phrase books are too preoccupied with attending to one's wants and generally "getting along" to pay much attention to what you should say once you have met someone. The following expressions have been tested for everyday conversational frequency and use, and, except for the rather special phrases at the end of the section, will be of immediate use for making conversation with anyone you meet.

Do you live in this city?
Abita in questa città?
AH-bee-ta een KWESS-ta cheet-TA?

Where are you from?
Da dove viene?
da DOH-veh V'YEH-neh?

I am from Milan.
Sono milanese.
SO-no mee-la-NEH-zeh.

Really?
Davvero?
dahv-VER-ro?

What a beautiful city!
Che bella città!
keh BEL-la cheet-TA!

I've been there.
La conosco.
la ko-NO-sko.

I would like to go there.
Mi piacerebbe andarvi.
mee p'ya'cheh-REB-beh ahn-DAR-vee.

How long have you been here?
Da quanto tempo è qui?
da KWAHN-toh TEM-po eh kwee?

For three days.
Da tre giorni.
da treh JOR-nee.

Several weeks.
Da parecchie settimane.
da pa-REK-k'yeh set-tee-MA-neh.

Two months.
Da due mesi.
da DOO-weh MEH-zee.

How long will you stay here?
Quanto tempo si ferma?
KWAHN-toh TEM-po see FAIR-ma?

I will stay for one month.
Resterò un mese.
reh-steh-RO oon MEH-zeh.

Have you been here before?
È già stato qui?
eh ja STA-toh kwee?

No, never.
No, mai.
no, my.

Once.
Una volta.
OO-na VOHL-ta.

Five years ago.
Cinque anni fa.
CHEEN-kweh AHN-nee fa.

Where are you living?
Dove abita?
DOH-veh AH-bee-ta?

At what hotel?
A quale albergo?
ah KWA-leh ahl-BAIR-go?

What do you think of Rome?
Che pensa di Roma?
keh PEN-sa dee RO-ma?

I like it very much.
Mi piace molto.
mee P'YA-cheh MOHL-toh.

It's very interesting.
È molto interessante.
eh MOHL-toh een-teh-res-SAHN-teh.

It's a beautiful city.
È una bella città.
eh OO-na BEL-la chee-TA.

The women are very beautiful.
Le donne sono molto belle.
leh DOHN-neh SO-no MOHL-toh BEL-leh.

Will you go to Florence?
Andrà a Firenze?
ahn-DRA ah fee-RENT-seh?

You must go there.
Deve andarci.
DEH-veh ahn-DAR-chee.

A proposito: When a person asks you whether you have been in certain places, you should be able to recognize the regional names, which usually resemble the English ones. Here are a few exceptions:

Venezia
veh-NEHTS-ya
Venice

il mezzogiorno
eel med-dzo-JOR-no
the south of Italy

il Trastevere
eel trahs-TEH-veh-reh
"The other side" of the
  Tiber, in Rome

Sicilia
see-CHEEL-ya
Sicily

Firenze
fee-RENT-seh
Florence

Do you come from the United States?
Lei viene dagli Stati Uniti?
lay V'YEH-neh DAHL-yee STA-tee oo-NEE-tee?

Yes, I am from New York.
Sì, sono di Nuova York.
*see, SO-no dee NWO-va
  york.*

I speak a little Italian.
Parlo un po'd'italiano.
*PAR-lo oon po dee-tahl-YA-
  no.*

But you have a good accent.
Ma Lei ha un buon accento.
*ma lay ah oon bwohn aht-
  CHEN-toh.*

You are very kind.
Lei è molto gentile.
*lay eh MOHL-toh jen-TEE-
  leh.*

Are you familiar with the United States?
Conosce gli Stati Uniti?
ko-NO-sheh l'yee STA-tee oo-NEE-tee?

Where have you been?
Dov'è stato?
doh-VEH STA-toh?

Do you like _____?
Le piace _____?
leh P'YA-cheh _____?

What do you think of _____?
Cosa pensa di _____?
Ko-za PEN-sa dee _____?

When people ask your opinion about something, you
will find the following comments most helpful.

It seems to me that . . .
Mi sembra che . . .
mee SEM-bra keh . . .

In any case . . .
In ogni caso . . .
een OHN-yee KA-zo . . .

Really?
Davvero?
dahv-VEH-ro?

What a shame!
Che peccato!
keh pek-KA-toh!

I don't know.
Non so.
nohn so.

I have forgotten.
Ho dimenticato.
oh dee-men-tee-KA-toh.

I agree.
Sono d'accordo.
SO-no dahk-KOR-doh.

You are right.
Ha ragione.
ah ra-JO-neh.

Is it possible?
È possibile?
eh pohs-SEE-bee-leh?

Very interesting.
Molto interessante.
MOHL-toh een-teh-res-SAHN-teh.

Magnificent.
Magnifico.
mahn-YEE-fee-ko.

Marvelous.
Meraviglioso.
meh-ra-veel-YO-zo.

Not bad.
Non è male.
nohn eh MA-leh.

Sometimes.
Qualche volta.
kwahl-keh VOHL-ta.

Never.
Mai.
my.

Often.
Spesso.
SPEHS-so.

You must come to see us.
Deve venire a trovarci.
DEH-veh veh-NEE-reh ah tro-VAR-chee.

At our house.
A casa nostra.
ah KA-za NO-stra.

With pleasure.
Con piacere.
kohn p'ya-CHEH-reh.

Are you married?
È sposato? (m)
eh spo-ZA-toh?
È sposata? (f)
eh spo-ZA-ta?

Do you have children?
Ha bambini?
ah bahm-BEE-nee?

No, I haven't.
No, non ne ho.
no, nohn neh oh.

Yes, I have.
Sì, ne ho.
see, neh oh.

How many girls?
Quante femmine?
KWAHN-teh FEM-mee-neh?

How many boys?
Quanti maschi?
KWAHN-tee MAHS-kee?

How old are they?
Quanti anni hanno?
*KWAHN-tee AHN-nee
  AHN-no?*

My son is seven years old.
Mio figlio has sette anni.
*MEE-yo FEEL-yo ah SET-
  teh AHN-nee.*

My daughter is ten years old.
Mia figlia ha dieci anni.
MEE-ya FEEL-ya ah D'YEH-chee AHN-nee.

What cute children!
Che bambini graziosi!
keh bahm-BEE-nee graht-YO-zee!

This is my . . .	**. . . mother.**	**. . . sister.**
Questa è mia . . .	. . . madre.	. . . sorella.
KWESS-ta eh	*. . . MA-dreh.*	*. . . so-REL-la.*
MEE-ya . . .		

. . . daughter.	**. . . wife.**	**. . . daughter-in-law.**
. . . figlia.	. . . moglie.	. . . nuora.
. . . FEEL-ya.	*. . . MOHL-yeh.*	*. . . NWO-ra.*

This is my . . .	**. . . father.**	**. . . brother.**
Questo è mio . . .	. . . padre.	. . . fratello.
KWESS-toh eh	*. . . PA-dreh.*	*. . . fra-TEL-lo.*
MEE-yo . . .		

... son.	... husband.	... son-in-law.
... figlio.	... marito.	... genero.
... FEEL-yo.	... ma-REE-toh.	... JEH-neh-ro.

Do you know ...	... **that man?**	... **Mr. Rossi?**
Conosce ...	... quell'uomo?	... il Signor Rossi?
ko-NO-sheh ...	... kwel-LWO-mo?	... eel SEEN-yor ROHS-see?

He is ...	... **a writer.**	... **an artist.**
Egli è ...	... uno scrittore.	... un artista.
EL-yee eh ...	... OO-no skree-TOH-reh.	... oon ar-TEES-ta.

... **a businessman.**	... **a lawyer.**	... **a doctor.**
... un uomo d'affari.	... un avvocato.	... un dottore.
... oon WO-mo dahf-FA-ree.	... oon ahv-vo-KA-toh.	... oon doht-TOH-reh.

... **a manufacturer.**	... **a military man.**	... **a painter.**
... un industriale.	... un militare.	... un pittore.
... oon een-doo-stree-YA-leh.	... oon mee-lee-TA-reh.	... oon peet-TOH-reh.

... **a banker.**	... **a professor.**	... **an actor.**
... un banchiere.	... un professore.	... un attore.
... oon bahnk-YEH-reh.	... oon pro-fes-SO-reh.	... oon aht-TOH-reh.

... **a member of the government.**	... **my husband.**
... un membro del governo.	... mio marito.
... oon MEHM-bro del go-VAIR-no.	... MEE-yo ma-REE-toh.

Do you know ...	... **that lady?**	... **Mrs. Martin?**
Conosce ...	... quella signora?	... la signora Martino?
ko-NO-sheh ...	... KWEL-la seen-YO-ra?	... la seen-YO-ra mar-TEE-no?

She is . . .	. . . a writer.	. . . a singer.
Ella è . . .	. . . una scrittrice.	. . . una cantante.
EL-la eh . . .	. . . *OO-na skreet-TREE-cheh.*	. . . *OO-na kahn-TAHN-teh.*

. . . a doctor.	. . . a teacher.
. . . una dottoressa.	. . . una maestra.
. . . *OO-na doht-toh-RES-sa.*	. . . *OO-na ma-EHS-tra.*

. . . an actress.	. . . my wife.
. . . un'attrice.	. . . mia moglie.
. . . *oon aht-TREE-cheh.*	. . . *MEE-ya MOHL-yeh.*

He is American.	She is American.
Egli è americano.	Ella è americana.
EL-yee eh ah-meh-ree-KA-no.	*EL-la eh ah-meh-ree-KA-na.*

He (she) is English.
Egli (ella) è inglese.
EL-yee (EL-la) eh een-GLEH-zeh.

He is Italian.	She is Italian.
Egli è italiano.	Ella è italiana.
EL-yee eh ee-tahl-YA-no.	*EL-la eh ee-tahl-YA-na.*

He (she) is very intelligent.
Egli (ella) è molto intelligente.
EL-yee (EL-la) eh MOHL-toh een-tel-lee-JEN-teh.

He is very nice.	She is very nice.
Egli è molto simpatico.	Ella è molto simpatica.
EL-yee eh MOHL-toh seem-PA-tee-ko.	*El-la eh MOHL-toh seem-PA-tee-ka.*

He (she) is very capable.
Egli (ella) è molto capace.
EL-yee (EL-la) eh MOHL-toh ka-PA-cheh.

This is my address.
Ecco il mio indirizzo.
EK-ko eel MEE-yo een-dee-REET-tso.

What is your address?
Qual'è il Suo indirizzo?
kwa-LEH eel SOO-wo een-dee-REET-tso?

Here is my telephone number.
Ecco il mio numero di telefono.
EK-ko eel MEE-yo NOO-meh-ro dee teh-LEH-fo-no.

What is your telephone number?
Qual'è il Suo numero di telefono?
kwa-LEH eel SOO-wo NOO-meh-ro dee teh-LEH-fo-no?

May I call you?
La posso chiamare?
la POHS-so k'ya-MA-reh?

When?
Quando?
KWAHN-doh?

Tomorrow morning.
Domani mattina.
doh-MA-nee maht-TEE-na.

Early.
Presto.
PRESS-toh.

In the afternoon.
Durante il pomeriggio.
doo-RAHN-teh eel po-meh-REED-jo.

My name is Richard.
Mi chiamo Riccardo.
mee K'YA-mo reek-KAR-doh.

What is your name?
Come si chiama?
KO-meh see K'YA-ma?

You dance very well.
Lei balla molto bene.
lay BAHL-la MOHL-toh BEH-neh.

You sing very well.
Lei canta molto bene.
lay KAHN-ta MOHL-toh BEH-neh.

A voice of an angel!
Una voce d'angelo!
OO-na VO-cheh D'AHN-jeh-lo!

What a pretty dress!
Che bel vestito!
keh bel vess-TEE-toh!

I have a surprise for you.
Ho una sorpresa per Lei.
oh OO-na sor-PREH-za pair lay.

Do you like it?
Le piace?
leh P'YA-cheh?

Can we see each other again?
Possiamo rivederci?
pohs-S'YA-mo ree-veh-DAIR-chee?

When?
Quando?
KWAHN-doh?

Where?
Dove?
DOH-veh?

What's the matter?
Cosa è successo?
KO-za eh soot-CHEHS-so?

Are you angry?
È arrabbiata? (to a woman)
eh ahr-rahb-B'YA-ta?
È arrabbiato? (to a man)
eh ahr-rahb-B'YA-toh?

Why?
Perchè?
pair-KEH?

I'm very sorry.
Mi dispiace molto.
Mee dees-P'YA-cheh MOHL-toh.

You are very beautiful.
Lei è molto bella.
lay eh MOHL-toh BEL-la.

You are very nice.
Lei è molto gentile. (to a man)
lay eh MOHL-toh jen-TEE-leh.
Lei è molto carina. (to a woman)
lay eh MOHL-toh ka-REE-na.

Where are you going?
Dove va?
DOH-veh va?

Let's go together.
Andiamo insieme.
ahnd-YA-mo een-S'YEH-meh.

I like you very much.
Ho molta simpatia per Lei.
oh MOHL-ta seem-pa-TEE-ya pair lay.

Are you serious?
Sul serio?
sool SEHR-yo?

And how do you feel?
E tu, cosa ne pensi?
eh too, KO-za neh PEN-see?

I (feel) the same.
Anch'io.
ahn-KEE-yo.

I love you.
Ti amo.
tee AH-mo.

Will you give me your photo?
Mi dai una tua foto?
mee dye OO-na TOO-wa FO-toh?

Will you write to me?
Mi scriverai?
mee skree-veh-RYE?

Don't forget!
Non dimenticare!
nohn dee-men-tee-KA-reh!

A proposito: In the last four sentences we have used the familiar form for *you*, **tu** instead of the more formal **Lei**, in its pronoun and verb forms, as the tone of the conversation implies a certain degree of familiarity. **Ti amo** means "I love you" and so does **Ti voglio bene.**

15. Words That Show You Are "With It"

There are certain words that Italian-speaking people use constantly but that do not always have an exact equivalent in English. To use them at the right time will make Italian people feel that you have good manners and are familiar with the most frequent Italian conversational phrases—in other words, that you are "with it." The Italian words and phrases are given first to make it easier for you to recognize them as they occur in everyday conversation.

We have divided these terms into two groups. The first is composed of selected polite expressions:

Bravo! (m) or **Brava!** (f)
BRA-vo!, BRA-va!
Good for you!

Congratulazioni!
kohn-gra-too-lahts-YO-nee!
Congratulations!

Complimenti!
kohm-plee-MEN-tee!
My compliments

Auguri!
ow-GOO-ree!
Best wishes!

Alla salute!
AHL-la sa-LOO-teh!
To your health!

Buon viaggio!
bwohn V'YAHD-jo!
Have a good trip!

Si diverta!
see dee-VAIR-ta!
Have a good time!

Saluti a ——— !
sa-LOO-tee ah — !
Regards to ——— !

Si accomodi!
see ahk-KO-mo-dee!
Make yourself comfortable!

To someone eating or about to eat:

Buon appetito!
bwohn ah-peh-TEE-toh!
Good appetite!

When someone sneezes:

Salute!
sa-LOO-teh!
Health!

To wish someone good luck:

Buona fortuna!   *(or)*   **In bocca al lupo!**
BWO-na for-TOO-na!   *een BOHK-ka ahl LOO-po!*
Good luck!   Into the mouth of the wolf!

                              To which one may reply:
                              Crepi il lupo!
                              KREH-pee eel LOO-po!
                              May the wolf burst!

Since the following phrases permeate conversation, it will interest you to know what they mean, as well as to learn to employ them as useful conversational stopgaps. The translations are quite free, as these expressions are very idiomatic.

Ma . . . !   **Così-così.**
ma . . . !   *ko-ZEE ko-ZEE.*
But . . . ! *or* Now, wait a   So-so.
minute!

Poi . . .   **Non è vero?**
poy . . .   *nohn eh VEH-ro?*
And then . . .   Isn't it? *or* Don't you think
                               so?

Più o meno.   **Andiamo!**
p'yoo oh MEH-no.   *ahnd-YA-mo!*
More or less.   Let's go! *or* Come on!

Vediamo un po'!   **Allora . . .**
vehd-YA-mo oon po!   *ah-LO-ra . . .*
Let's see!   Then . . .

Dai!   **Va bene!**
dye!   *va BEH-neh!*
Come on! Keep going!   It's okay!

Dunque . . .
DOON-kweh . . .
Well, now . . .

Ebbene . . .
eb-BEH-neh . . .
Well, now . . .

Cosa c'è di nuovo?
KO-za cheh dee N'WO-vo?
What's new?

Niente affatto.
N'YEN-teh ahf-FAHT-toh.
Nothing at all.

Ma no!
ma no!
You don't say! *or* Not at all!

Incredibile!
een-kreh-DEE-bee-leh!
Incredible!

C'è qualcosa che non va?
cheh kwahl-KO-za keh nohn va?
Is something wrong?

Va via!
va VEE-ya!
Go away!

Ma insomma . . .
ma een-SOHM-ma . . .
But after all . . .

Non fa niente!
nohn fa N'YEN-teh!
It doesn't matter!

Non vale la pena.
nohn VA-leh la PEH-na.
It's not worthwhile.

Favoloso!
fa-vo-LO-zo!
Great!

Fenomenale!
fe-no-meh-NA-leh!
Great!

Santo Cielo!
SAHN-toh CHEH-lo!
Good heavens!

Perbacco!
pair-BAHK-ko!
Good heavens! (literally "By Bacchus!")

Mamma mia!
MAHM-ma MEE-ya!
Good heavens! (literally "My mother!")

Si figuri!
see fee-GOO-ree!
Just imagine!

Shops in Italy still tend to be specialized, although there exist chains of general stores and even the supermarket—**supermercato**.

Names of Shops

Where can I find . . .
Dove posso trovare . . .
*DOH-veh POHS-so
tro-VA-reh . . .*

the department stores?
. . . i grandi magazzini?
. . . *ee GRAHN-dee ma-
gahd-DZEE-nee?*

. . . a dress shop?
. . . un negozio di
abbigliamento?
. . . *oon neh-GOHTS-yo dee
ahb-beel-ya-MEN-toh?*

. . . a hat shop?
. . . un negozio di cappelli?
. . . *oon neh-GOHTS-yo dee
kahp-PEL-lee?*

. . . a shoe store?
. . . un negozio di calzature?
. . . *oon neh-GOHTS-yo dee kahl-tsa-TOO-reh?*

. . . a perfume shop?
. . . una profumeria?
. . . *OO-na pro-foo-meh-
REE-ya?*

. . . a jewelry shop?
. . . una gioielleria?
. . . *OO-na joy-yel-leh-REE-
ya?*

. . . a drugstore?
. . . una farmacia?
. . . *OO-na far-ma-CHEE-
ya?*

. . . a bookshop?
. . . una libreria?
. . . *OO-na lee-breh-REE-
ya?*

. . . a toy shop?
. . . un negozio di giocattoli?
. . . *oon neh-GOHTS-yo dee
jo-KAHT-toh-lee?*

. . . a flower shop?
. . . un fioraio?
. . . *oon f'yo-RA-yo?*

... **an antique shop?**
... un negozio di antichità?
... *oon neh-GOHTS-yo dee ahn-tee-kee-TA?*

A grocery store?
... un negozio di
alimentari?
... *oon neh-GOHTS-yo dee*
ah-lee-men-TA-ree?

... **a market?**
... un mercato?
... *oon mair-KA-toh?*

... **a camera shop?**
... un negozio di articoli fotografici?
... *oon neh-GOHTS-yo dee ar-TEE-ko-lee fo-toh-GRA-*
fee-chee?

... **a tobacco shop?**
... una tabaccheria?
... *OO-na ta-bahk-keh-*
REE-ya?

... **a barber shop?**
... un barbiere?
... *oon barb-YEH-reh?*

... **a beauty shop?**
... un parrucchiere?
... *oon par-rook-K'YEH-reh?*

A proposito: Some additional shop signs you will see in Italy include **Gelateria** (ice cream parlor), **Salumeria** (a shop specializing in delicious sausages), and **Trattoria** (a small informal restaurant). In certain small shops **da** (at the house of) precedes a proper name. **Da Mario** means "at Mario's house" or "at Mario's shop."

General Shopping Vocabulary

May I help you?
Posso aiutarLa?
POHS-so ah-yoo-TAR-la?

What do you wish?
Che cosa desidera?
keh KO-za deh-ZEE-deh-ra?

I would like to buy . . .
Desidero comprare . . .
deh-ZEE-deh-ro kohm-PRA-reh . . .

. . . a gift for my husband.
. . . un regalo per mio marito.
. . . oon reh-GA-lo pair MEE-yo ma-REE-toh.

. . . a gift for my wife.
. . . un regalo per mia moglie.
. . . oon reh-GA-lo pair MEE-ya MOHL-yeh.

. . . something for a man.
. . . una cosa per uomo.
. . . OO-na KO-za pair WO-mo.

. . . something for a lady.
. . . una cosa per donna.
. . . OO-na KO-za pair DOHN-na.

Nothing for the moment.
Niente per ora.
N'YEN-teh pair OH-ra.

I'm just looking around.
Voglio solo guardare.
VOHL-yo SO-lo gwahr-DA-reh.

I'll be back later.
Torno più tardi.
TOR-no p'yoo TAR-dee.

I like this.
Mia piace questo.
mee P'YA-cheh KWESS-toh.

. . . that.
. . . quello.
. . . KWEL-lo.

How much is it?
Quanto costa?
KWAHN-toh KO-sta?

Show me another.
Me ne mostri un altro.
meh neh MO-stree oon AHL-tro.

Something less expensive.
Qualche cosa di meno costoso.
KWAHL-keh KO-za dee MEH-no ko-STO-zo.

Do you like this?
Le piace questo?
leh P'YA-cheh KWESS-toh?

May I try it on?
Posso provarlo?
POHS-so pro-VAR-lo?

That suits you marvelously.
Le sta benissimo.
leh sta beh-NEES-see-mo.

Good. I'll take it.
Va bene. Lo prendo.
va BEH-neh. lo PREN-doh.

Can you alter it?
Può fare delle riparazioni?
*pwo FA-reh DEL-leh ree-
pah-rahts-YO-nee?*

Is it handmade?
È fatto a mano?
eh FAHT-toh ah MA-no?

Is it hand-embroidered?
È ricamato a mano?
*eh ree-ka-MA-toh ah MA-
no?*

Will you wrap it?
Può incartarlo?
pwo een-kar-TAR-lo?

Can one pay by check?
Si può pagare con un
assegno?
*see pwo pa-GA-reh kohn oon
ahs-SEHN-yo?*

Can you send it to this address?
Può mandarlo a quest'indirizzo?
pwo mahn-DAR-lo ah kwest-een-dee-REET-tso?

A receipt, please.
Una ricevuta, per favore.
*OO-na ree-cheh-VOO-ta,
pair fa-VO-reh.*

The change, please.
Il resto, per favore.
*eel REHS-toh, pair fa-VO-
reh.*

Come see us again! Sale
Ritorni presto!   Svendita
ree-TOHR-nee   ZVEN-dee-ta
PRESS-toh!

Bargain sale!
Prezzi bassi!
*PRET-tsee BAHS-
see!*

POINT TO THE ANSWER

To make certain you and the salesperson understand the details, you may wish to use this "Point to the Answer" section. The sentence in Italian after the arrow asks the salesperson to point to the answer.

Per favore indiqui qui sotto la Sua risposta alla mia domanda. Molte grazie.

Non ne abbiamo.
We haven't any.

È tutto quello che abbiamo.
It's all we have.

Non ne abbiamo più grandi.
We haven't any larger.

Non ne abbiamo più piccoli.
We haven't any smaller.

Non mandiamo a casa.
We don't deliver.

Possiamo spedirlo in America.
We can send it to America.

Qual'è il Suo indirizzo?
What is your address?

Non accettiamo un assegno personale.
We don't accept personal checks.

Accettiamo assegni turistici.
We accept traveler's checks.

Clothes

a suit
un vestito
oon vess-TEE-toh

a coat
un cappotto
oon kahp-POHT-toh

a scarf
una sciarpa
OO-na SHAR-pa

a hat
un cappello
oon kahp-PEL-lo

gloves
guanti
GWAHN-tee

shoes
scarpe
SKAR-peh

boots
stivali
stee-VA-lee

an umbrella
un ombrello
oon ohm-BREL-lo

a raincoat
un impermeabile
*oon eem-pair-meh-
AH-bee-leh*

pajamas
un pigiama
oon pee-JA-ma

a bathrobe
una vestaglia
*OO-na vess-
TAHL-ya*

slippers
pantofole
pahn-TOH-fo-leh

a swimsuit
un costume da bagno
*oon ko-STOO-meh da
BAHN-yo*

sandals
sandali
SAHN-da-lee

a handkerchief
un fazzoletto
*oon-faht-tso-LET-
toh*

a blouse
una blusa
OO-na BLOO-za

a skirt
una gonna
OO-na GOHN-na

a handbag
una borsa
*OO-na
BOHR-sa*

stockings
calze
KAHLD-zeh

a slip
una sottoveste
*OO-na soht-
toh-VESS-
teh*

a brassiere
un regiseno
*oon red-jee-SEH-
no*

panties
mutandine
*moo-tahn-DEE-
neh*

a nightgown
una camicia da
notte
*OO-na ka-MEE-
cha da NOHT-
teh*

an evening dress
un vestito da sera
*oon vess-TEE-toh da
SEH-ra*

an evening coat
un cappotto da sera
*oon kahp-POHT-toh da
SEH-ra*

a shirt
una camicia
OO-na ka-MEE-cha

pants
i pantaloni
ee pahn-ta-LO-nee

a jacket
una giacca
OO-na JAHK-ka

a tie
una cravatta
OO-na kra-VAHT-ta

socks
i calzetti
ee kahld-ZET-tee

an undershirt
una canottiera
OO-na ka-noht-T'YEH-ra

undershorts
mutande
moo-TAHN-deh

Sizes—Colors—Material

What size?
Di che misura?
dee keh mee-SOO-ra?

small
piccolo, -a*
PEEK-ko-lo, -la

medium
medio, -a
MEHD-yo, -ya

large
grande
GRAHN-deh

extra large
extra grande
EX-tra GRAHN-deh

larger
più grande
p'yoo GRAHN-deh

smaller
più piccolo, -a
p'yoo PEEK-ko-lo, -la

wider
più largo, -a
p'yoo LAR-go, -ga

narrower
più stretto, -a
p'yoo STRET-toh, -ta

longer
più lungo, -a
p'yoo LOON-go, -ga

shorter
più corto, -a
p'yoo KOHR-toh, -ta

---

*If the article referred to is masculine (see dictionary) the adjective ends in **o**, if feminine, in **a**.

What color?
Di che colore?
dee keh ko-LO-reh?

red
rosso, -a
ROHS-so, -sa

blue
blu
bloo

yellow
giallo, -a
JAHL-lo, -la

orange
arancione
ah-rahn-CHO-neh

green
verde
VAIR-deh

violet
violetto, -a
v'yo-LET-toh, -ta

brown
marrone
mar-RO-neh

gray
grigio, -a
GREE-jo, ja

black
nero, -a
NEH-ro, -ra

white
bianco. -a
B'YAHN-ko, -ka

beige
beige
beige

darker
più scuro, -a
p'yoo SKOO-ro, -ra

lighter
più chiaro, -a
p'yoo K'YA-ro, -ra

Is it silk?
È di seta?
eh dee SEH-ta?

. . . linen?
. . . lino?
. . . *LEE-no?*

. . . velvet?
. . . velluto?
. . . *vel-LOO-toh?*

. . . wool?
. . . lana?
. . . *LA-na?*

. . . cotton?
. . . cotone?
. . . *ko-TOH-neh?*

. . . lace?
. . . merletti?
. . . *mair-LET-tee?*

. . . leather?
. . . cuoio?
. . . *KWO-yo?*

. . . suede?
. . . camoscio?
. . . *ka-MO-sho?*

. . . kid?
. . . pelle?
. . . *PEL-leh?*

. . . plastic?
. . . plastica?
. . . *PLAHS-tee-ka?*

. . . fur?
. . . pelliccia?
. . . *pel-LEET-cha?*

What kind of fur?
Che pelliccia è?
keh pel-LEET-cha eh?

fox
volpe
VOHL-peh

beaver
castoro
ka-STO-ro

seal	**mink**	**leopard**
foca	visone	leopardo
FO-ka	*vee-SO-neh*	*leh-oh-PAR-doh*

Newsstand

I would like . . .
Vorrei . . .
vor-RAY . . .

. . . a guide book
. . . una guida.
. . . *OO-na GWEE-da.*

. . . a map of the city.
. . . una mappa della città.
. . . *OO-na MAHP-pa DEL-la cheet-TA.*

. . . sunglasses.
. . . occhiali da sole.
. . . *ohk-K'YA-lee da SO-leh.*

. . . some postcards.
. . . delle cartoline.
. . . *DEL-leh kar-toh-LEE-neh.*

. . . this newspaper.
. . . questo giornale.
. . . *KWESS-toh jor-NA-leh.*

. . . that magazine.
. . . questa rivista.
. . . *KWESS-ta ree-VEE-sta.*

. . . a map of Italy.
. . . una mappa d'Italia.
. . . *OO-na MAHP-pa dee-TAHL-ya.*

. . . a newspaper in English.
. . . un giornale in inglese.
. . . *oon jor-NA-leh een een-GLEH-zeh.*

Tobacco Shop

Have you American cigarettes?
Ha delle sigarette americane?
ah DEL-leh see-ga-RET-teh ah-meh-ree-KA-neh?

cigars
sigari
SEE-ga-ree

a pipe
una pipa
OO-na PEE-pa

tobacco
tabacco
ta-BAHK-ko

matches
fiammiferi
f'yahm-MEE-feh-ree

a lighter
un accendisigaro
oon aht-chen-dee-SEE-ga-ro

a refill
un ricambio
oon ree-KAHMB-yo

Drugstore

I would like . . .
Vorrei . . .
vohr-RAY . . .

a toothbrush
uno spazzolino da denti
OO-na spaht-tso-LEE-no da DEN-tee

toothpaste
dentifricio
den-tee-FREE-cho

a razor
un rasoio
oon ra-ZOY-yo

razor blades
lamette
la-MET-teh

shaving cream
sapone da barba
sa-PO-neh da BAR-ba

cologne
colonia
ko-LOHN-ya

a hairbrush
una spazzola
OO-na SPAHT-tso-la

a comb
un pettine
oon pet-TEE-neh

aspirin
aspirina
ah-spee-REE-na

some iodine
dell'iodio
del-L'YOHD-yo

scissors
forbici
FOR-bee-chee

a nail file
una lima da unghie
*OO-na LEE-ma da OON-
ghee-yeh*

some antiseptic
dell'antisettico
del-lahn-tee-SET-tee-ko

Band-Aids
cerotti
cheh-ROHT-tee

cough drops
pastiglie per la tosse
pahs-TEEL-yeh pair la TOHS-seh

Cosmetics

I would like . . .
Vorei . . .
vohr-RAY . . .

powder
cipria
CHEEP-r'ya

lipstick
rossetto
rohs-SET-toh

eye shadow
ombretto
ohm-BRET-toh

nail polish
smalto
ZMAHL-toh

perfume
profumo
pro-FOO-mo

an eyebrow pencil
una matita per gli occhi
OO-na ma-TEE-ta pair l'yee OHK-kee

cotton
cotone
ko-TOH-neh

bobby pins
forcine
for-CHEE-neh

hair spray
lacca
LAHK-ka

Hairdresser

shampoo
uno shampù
OO-no shahm-POO

and set
e messa in piega
eh MEHS-sa een P'YEH-ga

a tint
una tintura
OO-na teen-TOO-ra

lighter
più chiara
p'yoo K'YA-ra

darker
più scura
p'yoo SKOO-ra

a manicure
una manicura
OO-na ma-nee-KOO-ra

a pedicure
una pedicura
OO-na peh-dee-KOO-ra

Barber

shave
barba
BAR-ba

and haircut
e capelli
eh ka-PEL-lee

a massage
un massaggio
oon mahs-SAHD-jo

Use scissors.
Usi le forbici.
OO-zee leh FOR-bee-chee.

shorter
più corto
p'yoo KOR-toh

not too short
non troppo corto
nohn TROHP-po KOR-toh

the top
il davanti
eel da-VAHN-tee

the back
il dietro
eel D'YEH-tro

the sides
i lati
ee LA-tee

That's fine.
Così va bene.
ka-ZEE va BEH-neh.

Where do I pay?
Dove devo pagare?
DOH-veh DEH-vo pa-GA-reh?

Food Market

I would like . . .
Vorrei . . .
vor-RAY . . .

. . . a dozen
. . . una dozzina
. . . *OO-na dohd-ZEE-na*

. . . of these.
. . . di questi.
. . . *dee KWESS-tee.*

. . . of those.
. . . di quelli.
. . . *dee KWEL-lee.*

I want five of them.
Ne voglio cinque.
neh VOHL-yo CHEEN-kweh.

Is this fresh?
È fresco questo?
eh FREH-sko KWESS-toh?

Three cans of this.
Tre barattoli di questo.
*treh ba-RAHT-toh-lee dee
    KWESS-toh.*

How much per kilo?
Quanto al chilo?
KWAHN-toh ahl KEE-lo?

**What kind of wine do you
    have?**
Che vino ha?
keh VEE-no ah?

All kinds.
Tutti.
TOOT-tee.

What is this?
Cos'è questo?
ko-ZEH KWESS-toh?

Please put it all in a bag.
Per favore metta tutto in un
    sacchetto.
*pair fa-VO-reh MET-ta
    TOOT-toh een oon sahk-
    KET-toh.*

A proposito: Weight is measured by the kilo—**chilo**—(kilogram—**chilogramma**) rather than by the pound. One kilo is equivalent to 2.2 pounds.

Jewelry

**I would like to
    see . . .**
Vorrei vedere . . .
*vor-RAY veh-
    DEH-reh . . .*

. . . a watch.
. . . un orologio.
*. . . oon oh-ro-
    LO-jo.*

. . . a ring.
. . . un anello.
*. . . oon ah-NEL-
    lo.*

. . . a necklace.
. . . una collana.
. . . OO-na kohl-LA-na.

. . . a bracelet.
. . . un braccialetto.
. . . oon braht-cha-LET-toh.

. . . some earrings
. . . degli orecchini.
. . . *DEL-yee oh-rehk-KEE-nee.*

Is this gold?	**. . . platinum?**	**. . . silver?**
È d'oro?	. . . di platino?	. . . d'argento?
eh DOH-ro?	. . . *dee PLA-tee-no?*	. . . *dar-JEN-toh?*

Is it silver-plated?	**Is it gold-plated?**
È argentato?	È dorato?
eh ar-jen-TA-toh?	*eh doh-RA-toh?*

a diamond	**a pearl**	**a ruby**
un brillante	una perla	un rubino
oon breel-LAHN-teh	*OO-na PAIR-la*	*oon roo-BEE-no*

a sapphire	**an emerald**
uno zaffiro	uno smeraldo
OO-no DZAHF-fee-ro	*OO-no zmeh-RAHL-doh*

Is this real?	**. . . or an imitation?**
È autentico?	. . . o un' imitazione?
eh ow-TEN-tee-ko?	. . . *oh oon ee-mee-tahts-YO-neh?*

Antiques

What period is this?	**It's beautiful.**
Di che epoca è questo?	È molto bello.
dee keh EH-po-ka eh KWESS-toh?	*eh MOHL-toh BEL-lo.*

But very expensive.	**How much is . . .**
Ma molto caro.	Quanto costa . . .
ma MOHL-toh KA-ro.	*KWAHN-toh KO-sta . . .*

. . . this book?
. . . questo libro?
. . . *KWESS-toh LEE-bro?*

. . . this picture?
. . . questo quadro?
. . . *KWESS-toh KWA-dro?*

. . . this map?
. . . questa mappa?
. . . *KWESS-ta MAHP-pa?*

. . . this frame?
. . . questa cornice?
. . . *KWESS-ta kor-NEE-cheh?*

. . . this piece of furniture?
. . . questo mobile?
. . . *KWESS-toh MO-bee-leh?*

Is it an antique?
È antico?
eh ahn-TEE-ko?

Can you ship it?
Può spedirlo?
pwo speh-DEER-lo?

To this address?
A questo indirizzo?
ah KWESS-toh een-dee-REET-tso?

17. Telephone

Talking on the phone is an excellent test of your ability to communicate in Italian because you can't see the person you are talking to, nor use gestures to help get across your meaning. When asking for someone, simply say his name and add **prego**. If you say the number instead of dialing, say the numbers in pairs: 3536 would be 35–36, or **trentacinque–trentasei**.

Where is the telephone?
Dov'è il telefono?
do-VEH eel teh-LEH-fo-no?

The telephone operator.
La telefonista.
la teh-leh-fo-NEES-ta.

Hello!
Pronto!
PROHN-toh!

Who is speaking?
Chi parla?
kee PAR-la?

Information.
Informazioni.
een-for-mahts-YO-nee.

Please, the telephone number of_____.
Per favore, il numero di telefono di _____.
*pair fa-VO-reh, eel NOO-meh-ro dee teh-LEH-fo-no
   dee _____.*

Long distance.
Interurbana.
een-tair-oor-BA-na.

Get me number _____ in Rome.
Mi dia il numero _____ a Roma.
mee DEE-ya eel NOO-meh-ro _____ ah RO-ma.

I would like to call New York, in the United States.
Vorrei chiamare Nuova York, negli Stati Uniti.
*vohr-RAY k'ya-MA-reh NWO-va york, NEL-yee STA-tee
   oo-NEE-tee.*

I am calling number _____.
Sto chiamando il numero _____.
sto k'ya-MAHN-doh eel NOO-meh-ro _____

Extension _____.
Interno _____.
een-TAIR-no _____

How long must I wait?
Quanto devo aspettare?
KWAHN-toh DEH-vo ahs-pet-TA-reh?

How much is it per minute?
Quanto costa al minuto?
KWAHN-toh KO-sta ahl mee-NOO-toh?

My number is _____.
Il mio numero è _____.
eel ME-yo NOO-meh-ro eh _____

Mr. (Mrs.) Rossi, please.
Il signor (la signora) Rossi, per piacere.
eel seen-YOR (la seen-YO-ra) ROHS-see, pair p'ya-CHEH-reh.

What?
Come?
Ko-meh?

He (she) isn't here.
Non c'è.
nohn cheh.

Hold on.
Attenda.
aht-TEN-da.

When is he (she) coming back?
Quando sarà di ritorno?
KWAHN-do sa-RA dee ree-TOR-no?

Very well, I'll call back.
Grazie, richiamerò.
GRAHTS-yeh, reek-ya-meh-RO.

Can I leave a message?
Posso lasciare un messaggio?
POHS-so la-SHA-reh oon mess-SAHD-jo?

Ask him (her) to call me.
Gli (le) dica di chiamarmi.
l'yee (leh) DEE-ka dee k'ya-MAR-mee.

I'll give you my number.
Le do il mio numero.
leh doh eel MEE-yo NOO-meh-ro.

This is Mr. Verga speaking.
Parla il signor Verga.
PAR-la eel seen-YOR VAIR-ga.

That is spelled V-E-R-G-A.
Si scrive V-E-R-G-A.
see SKREE-veh vee-eh-EHR-reh-jee-ah.

A	**B**	**B**	**D**
ah	*bee*	*chee*	*dee*

E	**F**	**G**	**H**
eh	*EF-feh*	*jee*	*AHK-ka*

I	**J**	**K**	**L**
ee	*ee-LOON-ga*	*KAHP-pa*	*el-LEH*

M	**N**	**O**	**P**
EM-meh	*EN-neh*	*oh*	*pee*

Q	**R**	**S**	**T**
koo	*EHR-reh*	*ES-seh*	*tee*

U	**V**	**W**	**X**
oo	*vee*	*DOHP-p'ya-vee*	*iks*

Y	**Z**
ee-GREH-ka	*DZAY-ta*

A proposito: As American and English names are often strange to Italian ears, you will find the spelled-out alphabet very useful for spelling your name when you leave a message.

Where is a public telephone?
Dov'è il telefono pubblico?
doh-VEH eel teh-LEH-fo-no POOB-blee-ko?

. . . the telephone book?
. . . l'elenco telefonico?
. . . leh-LEN-ko teh-leh-FO-nee-ko?

What do I put in?
Cosa metto dentro?
KO-za MET-toh DEN-tro?

How much do I owe you?
Quanto Le devo?
KWAHN-toh leh DEH-vo?

In Italy tokens are used in public telephones.

A token, please.
Un gettone, per favore.
oon jet-TOH-neh, pair fa-VO-reh.

Another token.
Un altro gettone.
oon AHL-tro jet-TOH-neh.

If there is no public telephone available:

May I use your phone?
Potrei usare il Suo telefono?
po-TRAY oo-ZA-reh eel SOO-wo teh-LEH-fo-no?

Certainly.
Certamente.
chair-ta-MEN-teh.

18. Post Office and Telegrams

One of the first things one does when abroad is to write postcards—**cartoline postale**—to friends and relatives. Here is how to mail them. You might also impress your friends by adding a few words in Italian, which you will find at the end of this section.

Where is the post office?
Dov'è la posta?
doh-VEH-la POHS-ta?

Ten stamps of one hundred lire.
Dieci francobolli da cento lire.
D'YEH-chee frahn-ko-BOHL-lee da CHEN-toh LEE-reh.

How much is needed?
Quanti ce ne vogliono?
KWAHN-tee cheh neh VOHL-yo-no?

... for air mail?
... per via aerea?
... pair VEE-ya ah-EH-reh-ya?

For a letter to the United States.
Per una lettera per gli Stati Uniti.
pair OO-na LEH-teh-ra pair l'yee STA-tee oon-NEE-tee.

... to England.
... per l'Inghilterra.
... pair leen-gheel-TEHR-ra.

... to Canada.
... per il Canada.
... pair eel ka-na-DA.

... to Spain.
... per la Spagna.
... pair la SPAHN-ya.

... to Germany.
... per la Germania.
... pair la jair-MAHN-ya.

to Yugoslavia.
... per la Jugoslavia.
... pair la yoo-go-SLAHV-ya.

... to France.
... per la Francia.
... pair la FRAHN-cha.

. . . to Austria.
. . . per l'Austria.
. . . *pair L'OW-stree-ya.*

. . . to Greece.
. . . per la Grecia.
. . . *pair la GREH-cha.*

For names of other countries, see dictionary.

a registered letter
una lettera raccomandata
OO-na LET-teh-ra rahk-ko-mahn-DA-ta

an insured parcel
un pacco assicurato
oon PAHK-ko ahs-see-koo-RA-toh

Where can I send a telegram?
Dove posso mandare un
  telegramma?
DOH-veh POHS-so mahn-DA-reh oon tel-leh-GRAHM-ma?

a fax . . .
oon fax . . .
a fax . . .

How much is it per word?
Quanto costa alla parola?
KWAHN-toh KO-sta AHL-la pa-RO-la?

I need writing paper . . .
Ho bisogno di carta da
  lettere . . .
oh bee-ZOHN-yo dee KAR-ta da LET-teh-reh.

. . . envelopes.
. . . di buste.
. . . dee BOO-steh.

Can you lend me . . .
Mi può imprestare . . .
mee pwo eem-pres-TA-reh . . .

. . . a pen?
. . . una penna?
. . . OO-na PEN-na?

. . . a pencil?
. . . una matita?
. . . OO-na ma-TEE-ta?

Postcards

Dear John,
Caro Giovanni,

Greetings from Florence.
Saluti da Firenze.

I'm having a fine time here.
Mi diverto molto qui.

I hope to see you soon.
Spero di rivederLa presto.

Best wishes to all,
Saluti a tutti,

Dear Jane,
Cara Giovanna.

Regards from Naples.
Ricordi da Napoli.

It's very beautiful here.
E molto bello qui.

But I miss you,
Ma sento la Sua mancanza.

Till soon.   **Fondly,**
A presto.   Caramente,

19. The Weather

---

winter
l'inverno
leen-VAIR-no

spring
la primavera
la pree-ma-VEH-ra

summer
l'estate
leh-STA-teh

autumn
l'autunno
low-TOON-no

How is the weather?
Com'è il tempo?
ko-MEH eel TEM-po?

The weather is fine.
È bel tempo.
eh bel TEM-po.

It's cold.
Fa freddo.
fa FRED-doh.

It's raining.
Piove.
P'YO-veh.

I need an umbrella.
Ho bisogno di un ombrello.
oh bee-ZOHN-yo dee oon ohm-BREL-lo.

. . . a raincoat.
. . . un impermeabile.
. . . oon eem-pair-mee-AH-bee-leh.

. . . boots.
. . . stivali.
. . . stee-VA-lee.

It's snowing.
Nevica.
neh-VEE-ka.

Do you like to ski? . . . to skate?
Le piace sciare? . . . pattinare?
leh P'YA-cheh . . . paht-tee-NA-
SHAH-reh? reh?

I want to rent a pair of skis. . . . skates.
Desidero affitare un paio di sci. . . . pattini.
deh-ZEE-deh-ro ahf-fee-TA- . . . PAHT-tee-nee.
reh oon PA-yo dee shee.

It's very hot.
Fa molto caldo.
fa MOHL-toh KAHL-doh.

Let's go swimming.
Andiamo a nuotare.
ahnd-YA-mo ah nwo-TA-reh.

119

Where is the beach?
Dov'è la piaggia?
doh-VEH la P'YA-ja?

Where is the pool?
Dov'è la piscina?
doh-VEH la pee-SHEE-na?

I want to rent a small boat.
Desidero affitare una batello.
deh-ZEE-deh-ro ahf-fee-TA-reh OO-na ba-TEL-lo.

. . . a surfboard.
. . . una tavoletta da surf.
. . . OO-na ta-vo-LEHT-ta da soorf.

. . . a mask and fins.
. . . una maschera e pinne.
. . . OO-na MA-skeh-ra eh PEEN-neh.

. . . air tanks.
. . . delle bombole d'aria.
. . . DEHL-leh BOHM-bo-leh DAR-ya.

Is it safe to swim here?
È sicuro nuotare qui?
eh see-KOO-ro nwo-TA-reh kwee?

Are there sharks?
Ci sono pescecani?
chee SO-no peh-sheh-KA-nee?

What is that big ship on the horizon?
Qual è quel grande vapore sul horizonte.
Kwahl eh kwel grahn-deh va-PO-reh sool oh-ree-ZOHN-teh?

Is it a cargo ship?
È un vapore merce?
eh oon va-PO-reh MEHR-cheh?

No, it isn't.
No, non è.
no, nohn eh.

It's a passenger ship.
È un vapore di passagieri.
eh oon va-PO-reh dee pahs-sa-J'YEH-ree.

It travels to Greece, Turkey . . .
Viaggia a Grecia, Turchia,
V'YAJ-ja ah GREY-cha, Toor-KEE-ya,

Egypt and the Island of the Mediterranean.
al Egitto e alle isole del Mediterraneo.
ahl eh-jeet-toh eh AHL-leh EE-so-leh del meh-dee-tehr-RA-neh-yo.

But look at that beautiful yacht over there!
Ma veda qual bellisimo at la-giù!
ma VEH-da k'wahl bel-LEE-see-mo yaht la-JOO!

I can't read the name . . .
Non posso leggere il nome . . .
nohn POHS-so LEJ-jeh-reh eel NO-meh . . .

Wait, I can see it with my binoculars.
Aspetti, posso vederlo con binoculo.
ahs-PET-tee, POHS-so veh-dehr-lo con bee-NO-ku-lo

It's called "La Dolce Vita."*
Si chiama "La Dolce Vita."
see K'YA-ma la DOHL-cheh VEE-ta.

---

*"The Sweet (or soft) Life"

20. Doctor and Dentist

Doctor

I am ill.
Mi sento male.
mee SEN-toh MA-leh.

My wife . . .
Mia moglie . . .
MEE-ya MOHL-yeh . . .

My husband . . .
Mio marito . . .
MEE-yo ma-REE-toh . . .

My daughter . . .
Mia figlia . . .
MEE-ya FEEL-ya . . .

My son . . .
Mio figlio . . .
MEE-yo FEEL-yo . . .

My friend . . .
Il mio amico (m) . . .
eel MEE-yo ah-MEE-ko . . .
La mia amica (f) . . .
la MEE-ya ah-MEE-ka . . .

. . . is ill.
. . . si sente male.
. . . see SEN-teh MA-leh.

We need a doctor.
C'è bisogno di un dottore.
cheh bee-ZOHN-yo dee oon doht-TOH-reh.

When can he come?
Quando può venire?
KWAHN-doh pwo veh-NEE-reh?

Well, what's wrong with you?
Allora, cosa succede?
ahl-LO-ra, ko-za soot-CHEH-deh?

I don't feel well.
Non mi sento bene.
nohn mee SEN-toh BEH-neh.

Where does it hurt?
Dove Le fa male?
DOH-veh leh fa MA-leh?

Here.
Qui.
kwee.

I have a pain . . .
Ho mal . . .
oh mahl . . .

He (she) has a pain . . .
Lui (lei) ha mal . . .
lwee (lay) ah mahl . . .

. . . in the head.
. . . di testa.
. . . *dee TEH-sta.*

. . . in the throat.
. . . di gola.
. . . *dee GO-la.*

. . . in the ear.
. . . d'orecchio.
. . . *doh-REHK-kee-oh.*

. . . in the stomach.
. . . di stomaco.
. . . *dee STO-ma-ko.*

. . . in the back.
. . . di schiena.
. . . *dee SK'YEH-na.*

I hurt my leg.
Mi sono fatto male alla gamba.
mee SO-no FAHT-toh MA-leh AHL-la GAHM-ba.

. . . my foot.
. . . al piede.
. . . *ahl P'YEH-deh.*

. . . my arm.
. . . al braccio.
. . . *ahl BRAHT-cho.*

. . . my hand.
. . . alla mano.
. . . *AHL-la MA-no.*

I am dizzy.
Mi gira la testa.
mee JEE-ra la TEH-sta.

I can't sleep.
Non posso dormire.
nohn POHS-so dor-MEE-reh.

I have a fever.
Ho la febbre.
oh la FEB-breh.

I have diarrhea.
Ho la diarrea.
oh la dee-yar-REH-ya.

Since when?
Da quando?
da KWAHN-doh?

Since yesterday.
Da ieri.
da YEH-ree.

Since two days ago.
Da due giorni.
da DOO-weh JOR-nee.

What have you eaten?
Che cosa ha mangiato?
keh KO-za ah mahn-JA-toh?

Undress.
Si spogli.
see SPOHL-yee.

Lie down.
Si distenda.
see dee-STEN-da.

Sit up.
Si sieda.
see S'YEH-da.

Breathe deeply.
Respiri a fondo.
reh-SPEE-ree ah FOHN-doh.

Open your mouth.
Apra la bocca.
AH-pra la BOHK-ka.

Show me your tongue.
Mi mostri la lingua.
mee MO-stree la LEEN-gwa.

Cough.
Tossisca.
tohs-SEES-ka.

Say "thirty-three."
Dica "trentatrè."
DEE-ka TRAIN-ta-treh.

Get dressed.
Si vesta.
see VEH-sta.

You must stay in bed.
Deve stare a letto.
DEH-veh STA-reh ah LET-toh.

You must go to the hospital.
Deve andare all'ospedale.
DEH-veh ahn-DA-reh ahl-lo-speh-DA-leh.

Take this prescription.
Prenda questa ricetta.
PREN-da KWESS-ta ree-CHET-ta.

Take these pills.
Prenda queste pastiglie.
PREN-da KWESS-teh pa-STEEL-yeh.

Is it serious?
È grave?
eh GRA-veh?

It's not serious.
Non è grave.
nohn eh GRA-veh.

Don't worry.
Non si preoccupi.
nohn see preh-OHK-koo-pee.

You have . . .
Lei ha . . .
lay ah . . .

. . . indigestion.
. . . un indigestione.
. . . oon een-dee-jest-YO-neh.

. . . an infection.
. . . un'infezione.
. . . oon-een-fehts-YO-neh.

. . . a cold.
. . . un raffred-dore.
. . . oon rahf-fred-DOR-reh.

. . . liver trouble.
. . . mal di fegato.
. . . mahl dee FEH-ga-toh.

. . . appendicitis.
. . . l'appendicite.
. . . la-pen-dee-CHEE-teh.

. . . a heart attack.
. . . un attacco cardiaco.
. . . oon aht-TAHK-ko kard-
EE-ah-ko.

Be careful.
Stia attento.
STEE-ya aht-TEN-toh.

Don't eat too much.
Non mangi troppo.
nohn MAHN-gee TROHP-po.

Don't drink any alcoholic drinks.
Non prenda bevande alcooliche.
nohn PREN-da beh-VAHN-deh ahl-ko-OH-lee-keh.

Except wine, of course.
Eccetto il vino,
  naturalmente.
et-CHET-toh eel VEE-no,
na-too-rahl-MEN-teh.

How do you feel today?
Come si sente oggi?
KO-meh see SEN-teh OHD-
jee?

The same.
Lo stesso.
lo STES-so.

Better.
Meglio.
MEHL-yo.

Much better.
Molto meglio.
MOHL-toh
MEHL-yo.

A proposito: The Centigrade scale is also used to measure body temperature. The normal body temperature is 36.7 degrees. So if you have anything higher than that, you have a fever—**Lei ha febbre**.

Dentist

In the unlikely event that the dentist should hurt you, tell him **Si fermi!**—"Stop!"—or **Aspetti un momento!**—"Wait a moment!" This will give you time to regain your courage.

Can you recommend a dentist?
Può raccomandarmi un dentista?
pwo rahk-ko-mahn-DAR-mee oon den-TEES-ta?

I have a toothache.
Ho mal di denti.
oh mahl dee DEN-tee.

It hurts here.
Mi fa male qui.
mee fa MA-leh kwee.

You need a filling.
Ha bisogno di un'otturatura.
ah bee-ZOHN-yo dee oon-oht-too-ra-TOO-ra.

Just fix it temporarily.
Me lo aggiusti provvisoriamente.
meh lo ahd-JOO-stee prohv-vee-zohr-ya-MEN-teh.

How long will it take?
Quanto tempo ci vuole?
KWAHN-toh TEM-po chee VWO-leh?

A few minutes.
Pochi minuti.
PO-kee mee-NOO-tee.

There is an infection.
C'è un'infezione.
cheh oon-een-fehts-YO-neh.

I must extract this tooth.
Dobbiamo togliere questo dente.
dohb-B'YA-mo TOHL-yeh-reh KWESS-toh DEN-teh.

An anesthetic, please.
Per favore, un anestetico.
pair fa-VO-reh, oon ah-nes-TEH-tee-ko.

Does it hurt?	**A little.**	**Not at all.**
Fa male?	Un poco.	Per niente.
fa MA-leh?	*oon PO-ko.*	*pair N'YEN-teh.*

Is it finished?
È finito?
eh fee-NEE-toh?

How much do I owe you?
Quanto le devo?
KWAHN-toh leh DEH-vo?

21. Problems and Police

Although the situations suggested below may never happen to you, the words are useful to know, just in case.

Go away!
Vada via!
VA-da VEE-ya!

Leave me alone!
Mi lasci in pace!
mee LA-shee een PA-cheh!

I'll call a policeman.
Chiamo la polizia.
K'YA-mo la po-leet-SEE-ya.

Police!
Guardia!
GWAHRD-ya!

Help!
Aiuto!
ah-YOO-toh!

What's going on?
Cosa succede?
KO-za soot-CHEH-deh?

This person is annoying me.
Questa persona non mi lascia in pace.
KWESS-ta pair-SO-na nohn mee LA-sha een PA-cheh.

Where is the police station?
Dov'è la stazione di polizia?
doh-VEH la stahts-YO-neh dee po-leet-SEE-ya.

I have been robbed of . . .
Mi hanno rubato . . .
mee AHN-no roo-BA-toh . . .

. . . my wallet.
. . . il portafoglio.
. . . eel por-ta-FOHL-yo.

. . . my watch.
. . . l'orologio.
. . . lo-ro-LO-jo.

. . . jewelry.
. . . i gioielli.
. . . ee joy-YEL-lee.

. . . my suitcase.
. . . la valigia.
. . . la va-LEE-ja.

. . . my car.
. . . la macchina.
. . . la MAHK-kee-na.

I've lost my passport!
Ho perduto il mio passaporto!
oh pehr-DOO-toh eel MEE-yo pahs-sa-POR-toh!

Stop that man!
Fermate quell'uomo!
fair-MA-teh kwel-LWO-mo!

He's the thief.
È lui il ladro.
eh lwee eel LA-dro.

I am innocent.
Sono innocente.
SO-no een-no-CHEN-teh.

I haven't done anything.
Non ho fatto niente.
nohn oh FAHT-toh N'YEN-
    teh.

I don't recognize him.
Non lo riconosco.
nohn lo ree-ko-NOHS-ko.

I need a lawyer.
Voglio un avvocato.
VOHL-yo oon ahv-vo-KA-
    toh.

Notify the American Consul.
Notifichi il console americano.
no-TEE-fee-kee eel KOHN-so-leh ah-meh-ree-KA-no.

It's a misunderstanding.
È un malinteso.
eh oon ma-leen-TEH-zo.

Don't worry.
Non si preoccupi.
nohn see preh-OHK-koo-pee.

Can I go now?
Posso andare ora?
POHS-so ahn-DA-reh OH-ra?

Of course.
Certo.
CHEHR-toh.

Everything is all right.
Tutto va bene.
TOOT-toh va BEH-neh.

Return to the hotel.
Ritorni al all'behr-go.
ree-TOR-nee ahl ahl'BEHR-go.

What did you have in your purse?
Cosa aveva nella bolsa?
KO-sa ah-VEH-va NEHL-la BOHL-sa?

We will find your property.
Troveremo la Sua proprietà.
tro-va-REH-mo la SOO-ah pro-pree-yeh-TA.

Wait for our call.
Aspetti la nostra chiamata.
Ah-SPET-tee la NO-stra K'ya-MA-ta.

We will call soon.
Chiamaremo presto.
kya-ma-REH-mo PRESS-toh.

Everything will be O.K.
Tutto andrà bene.
TOO-toh ahn-DRA BEH-neh.

The expressions in this section will help you enjoy a game of
calcio (soccer), **corse di cavalli** (horse races), or other sports
or spectacles you may encounter in Italy. To ask "Who is
winning?" one says **Chi vince?** (*kee VEEN-cheh*) and "Who
won?" is **Chi ha vinto?** (*kee ah VEEN-toh*). To express ap-
proval you shout **Bravo!** (*BRA-vo*) or **Brava!** for a woman
performer. If you win at the races it is "good fortune"—
Buona fortuna! (*BWO-na for-TOO-na*) and if one loses, one
may say **Peccato!** (*pek-KA-toh*) meaning a "shame" or "sin."

Do you like tennis?
Le piacce il tennis?
lay P'YA-cheh eel TEH-neess?

I like to play it . . .
Mi piacce giocarlo . . .
meh P'YA-cheh jo-KAR-lo . . .

and I like to see it played . . .
y mi piace vederlo giocatto . . .
ee meh P'YA-cheh veh-DEHR-lo jo-KA-toh . . .

but it's easier to watch it.
ma è più facile osservarlo.
ma eh p'yoo FA-chee-leh ohs-sehr-VAR-lo.

I would like to see a soccer game.
Io vorrei vedere una partite di calcio.
*EE-yo vo-RRAY veh-DEH OO-na par-TEE-teh dee
KAHL-tz'yo.*

There will be a big game Sunday . . .
Ci sarà una partita importante domenica . . .
*chee sa-RA OO-na par-TEE-ta eem-por-TAHN-teh doh-
MEH-nee-ka . . .*

. . . Milan against Turin.
. . . Milano contra Torino.
. . . mee-LA-no KOHN-tra toh-REE-no.

One says that Turin will win.
Si dice che Torino vincerà.
se DEE-cheh keh toh-REE-no veen-cheh-RA.

Today we can go to the horse races.
Oggi possiamo andare alle corse di cavallo.
*OHJ-jee pohs-S'YA-mo ahn-DA-reh AHL-leh KOR-seh
dee ka-VAHL-o.*

Which horse is the favorite?
Qual'è il cavallo favorito?
KWA-leh eel ka-VAHL-lo fa-vo-REE-toh?

They say that Nero will win.
Diconno che Nerone vincerà.
DEE-ko-no keh neh-RO-neh veen-cheh-RA.

Where can we place a bet?
Dove possiamo fare una scommessa?
DOH-veh pohs-S'YA-mo FA-reh OO-na sko-MEHS-sa?

Over there in front of the grandstand.
La-giù davanti alla tribuna.
la-JOO da-VAHN-tee AHL-la tree-BOO-na.

Please, put this on Nerone, to win.
Per favore metta questo su Nerone, per vincere.
*pair fa-VO-reh MET-ta KWESS-toh soo neh-RO-neh, pair
VEEN-cheh-reh.*

Would you like to see a car race?
Vorebbe vedere una corsa di maquine?
*vo-REB-beh veh-DEH-reh OO-na KOR-sa dee MA-kee-
neh?*

It's very popular here.
Quì è molto populare.
kwee eh MOOL-toh po-poo-LA-reh.

It's exciting but it's dangerous, isn't it?
Emozionante ma è pericoloso, non è vero?
*eh-moht-s'yo-NAHN-teh ma eh peh-ree-ko-LO-so, nohn eh
    VEH-ro?*

Yes, there are frequent accidents . . .
Sì, ci sono frecuentemente incidenti . . .
*see, chee so-no freh-kwen-teh-MEN-teh een-chee-DEN-
teh . . .*

. . . but that is part of the sport.
. . . ma quello fa parte dello sport.
. . . ma KWEL-lo fa PAR-teh DEHL-lo sport.

It's like the chariot races . . .
È como i corsi di carri . . .
eh KO-mo ee KOR-see dee KA-rree . . .

. . . in the times of Ancient Rome!
. . . nei tempi della Roma antica!
. . . nay TEM-pee DEHL-la RO-ma ahn-TEE-ka!

23. Housekeeping

The following chapter will be especially interesting for those who plan to stay longer in Italy or have occasion to employ Italian-speaking baby-sitters or household help, abroad or even at home.

What is your name?
Come si chiama?
KO-meh see K'YA-ma?

Where did you work before?
Dove ha lavorato prima?
DOH-veh ah la-vo-RA-toh PREE-ma?

Can you take care of a baby?
È capace di curare un bambino?
eh ka-PA-cheh dee koo-RA-reh oon bahm-BEE-no?

Can you cook?
Può cucinare?
pwo koo-chee-NA-reh?

We will pay you _____ lire per week.
La pagheremo _____ lire ogni settimana.
la pa-gheh-REH-mo _____ lee-reh OHN-yee set-tee-MA-na.

Thursday will be your day off.
Giovedì è il suo giorno di libertà.
jo-veh-DEE eh eel SOO-wo JOR-no dee lee-bair-TA.

This is your room.
Questa è la sua stanza.
KWESS-ta eh la SOO-wa STAHNT-sa.

Please clean . . .
Per favore pulisca . . .
pair fa-VO-reh poo-LEES-ka . . .

. . . the living room.
. . . la sala di soggiorno.
. . . la SA-la dee sohd-JOR-no.

. . . the dining room.
. . . la sala da pranzo.
. . . la SA-la da PRAHNT-so.

. . . the bedroom.
. . . la stanza da letto.
. . . la STAHNT-sa da LET-toh.

. . . the bathroom.
. . . il bagno.
. . . eel BAHN-yo.

. . . the kitchen.
. . . la cucina.
. . . la koo-CHEE-na.

Wash the dishes.
Lavi i piatti.
LA-vee ee P'YAHT-tee.

Sweep the floor.
Scopi il pavimento.
SKO-pee eel pa-vee-MEN-toh.

Use the vacuum cleaner.
Usi l'aspirapolvere.
OO-zee la-spee-ra-POHL-veh-reh.

. . . the broom.
. . . la scopa.
. . . la SKO-pa.

Polish the silver.
Lucidi l'argenteria.
LOO-chee-dee lar-jen-teh-REE-ya.

Make the beds.
Faccia i letti.
FAHT-cha ee LET-tee.

Change the sheets.
Cambi le lenzuola.
KAHM-bee leh lend-ZWO-la.

Wash this.
Lavi questo.
LA-vee KWESS-toh.

Iron this.
Stiri questo.
STEE-ree KWESS-toh.

Have you finished?
Ha finito?
ah fee-NEE-toh?

What do you need?
Di che cosa ha bisogno?
dee keh KO-za ah bee-ZOHN-yo?

Go to the market.
Vada al mercato.
VA-da ahl mair-KA-toh.

Here is the list.
Ecco la lista.
EK-ko la LESS-ta.

Put the milk in the refrigerator.
Metta il latte nel frigorifero.
MET-ta eel LAHT-teh nel free-go-REE-feh-ro.

If someone calls, write the name here.
Se qualcuno chiama, scriva il nome qui.
seh kwahl-KOO-no K'YA-ma, SKREE-va eel NO-meh kwee.

I'll be at this number.
Sarò a questo numero.
sa-RO ah KWESS-toh NOO-meh-ro.

I'll be back at four o'clock.
Tornerò alle quattro.
tor-neh-RO AHL-leh KWAHT-tro.

Feed the baby at _____ o'clock.
Dia da mangiare al bambino alle _____.
DEE-ya da mahn-JA-reh ahl bahm-BEE-no AHL-leh _____.

Give the child a bath.
Faccio il bagno al bambino.
FAHT-cha eel BAHN-yo ahl bahm-BEE-no.

Put him to bed at eight.
Lo metta a letto alle otto.
lo MET-ta ah LET-toh AHL-leh OHT-toh.

Serve lunch at two o'clock.
Serva la colazione alle due.
SAIR-va la ko-lahts-YO-neh AHL-leh DOO-weh.

Did anyone telephone?
Ha telefonato qualcuno?
ah teh-leh-fo-NA-toh kwahl-KOO-no?

We are having guests for dinner.
Abbiamo ospiti a pranzo.
ahb-B'YA-mo OH-spee-tee ah PRAHNT-so.

Set the table for eight.
Prepari la tavola per otto.
preh-PA-ree la TA-vo-la pair OHT-toh.

Put these flowers on the table.
Metta questi fiori sulla tavola.
MET-ta KWESS-tee F'YO-ree SOOL-la TA-vo-la.

Serve dinner at nine o'clock.
Serva il pranzo alle nove.
SAIR-va eel PRAHNT-so AHL-leh NO-veh.

There's someone at the door.
C'è qualcuno alla porta.
cheh kwahl-KOO-no AHL-la POR-ta.

Open it, please.
Apra per favore.
AH-pra pair fa-VO-reh.

24. Some Business Phrases

You will find the short phrases and vocabulary in this section extremely useful if you are on a business trip to Italy. While it is true that English is a prominent foreign language in Italy and that efficient interpreters are available, these phrases will add another dimension to your contacts with your Italian business associates. The fact that you have made the effort to master some business expressions will be a compliment to your hosts and will indicate that you, by using some phrases in their language, are reciprocating their traditional politeness.

Good morning. Is Mr. Tassiano in?
Buongiorno. C'è il signor Tassiano?
bwohn-JOR-no. cheh eel seen-YOR Tahss-YA-no?

I have an appointment.
Ho un appuntamento.
oh oon ahp-poon-ta-MEN-toh.

Here is my card.
Ecco il mio biglietto da visita.
EHK-ko eel MEE-yo beel-YET-toh da vee-ZEE-ta.

Thank you. He is expecting you.
Grazie. Lo sta aspettando.
GRAHTS-yeh. lo sta ah-spet-TAHN-doh.

This way, please.
Da questa parte, prego.
da KWESS-ta PAR-teh, PREH-go.

Welcome to Italy, Mr. Brown.
Benvenuto in Italia, signor Brown.
ben-veh-NOO-toh een ee-TAHL-ya, seen-YOR Brown.

Do you like Milan?
Le piace Milano?
leh P'YA-cheh Mee-LA-no?

Very much. It's a marvelous city.
Moltissimo. È una città meravigliosa.
mohl-TISS-see-mo. eh OO-na cheet-TA meh-ra-veel-YO-za.

We understand that . . .
Sappiamo che . . .
sahp-P'YA-mo keh . . .

. . . you are interested in our cars.
Lei è interessato nelle nostra macchine.
lay eh een-teh-ress-SA-toh NEHL-leh NOHS-tro MAHK-kee-neh.

Here is our latest catalog.
Ecco il nostro ultimo catalogo.
EHK-ko eel NOHS-tro ca-TA-lo-go.

It shows all our new models,
Mostra tutti i nostri modelli nuovi,
MOHS-tra TOOT-tee ee NOHS-tree mo-DEL-lee NWO-vee,

limousines, sedans, convertibles,
limousine, berline, decapottabili,
lee-moo-ZEE-neh, behr-LEE-neh, deh-ca-poht-TA-bee-lee,

and sports cars.
e macchine sportive.
eh MAHK-kee-neh spor-TEE-veh.

Thank you.
Grazie.
GRAHTS-yeh.

That's just what I need.
E proprio ciò di cui ho bisogno.
eh PRO-pree-yo cho dee kwee oh bee-SOHN-yo.

Would you like to visit our factory?
Desidera visitare la nostra fabbrica?
deh-zee-DEH-ra vee-zee-TA-reh la NOHS-stra FAHB-bree-ka?

An excellent idea!
È un'ottima idea!
eh oo-NOHT-tee-ma ee-DEH-ya!

You are very kind.
È molto gentile.
eh MOHL-toh jen-TEE-leh.

It was a pleasure to visit your factory.
È stato un piacere vistare la sua fabbrica.
eh STA-toh oon p'ya-CHEH-reh vee-zee-TA-reh la SOO-wa FAHB-bree-ka.

It's a very efficient factory.
È una fabbrica molto efficiente.
eh OO-na FAHB-ree-ka MOHL-toh ef-fee-CHEN-teh.

We would like to place an order.
Voremmo fare un'ordinazione.
vor-REH-mo FA-reh oo-nor-dee-na-T'SYO-neh.

We expect a discount of _____ percent.
Ci aspettiamo uno sconto del _____ percento.
chee ah-spet-T'YA-mo OO-no SCOHN-toh del _____ pehr CHEN-toh.

What are the terms of payment?
Quali sono i termini di pagamento?
KWA-lee SO-no ee TAIR-mee-nee dee pa-ga-MEN-toh?

By bank draft of 30 days, 60 days, 90 days.
Con tratta bancaria di trenta giorni, sesanta giorni, novanta giorni.
cohn TRAHT-ta bahn-CAR-ya dee TREN-ta JOR-nee, seh-SAN-ta JOR-nee, no-VAHN-ta JOR-nee.

Irrevocable letter of credit.
Lettera di credito irrevocabile.
let-TEH-ra dee creh-DEE-toh eer-reh-vo-CA-bee-leh.

Within how many days can we expect shipment?
Fra quanti giorni si può aspettare la consegna?
*fra KWAHN-tee JOR-nee see pwo ah-spet-TAR-eh la con-
SEHN-ya?*

Are these your best terms?
Sono questi i suoi migliori termini?
SO-no KWESS-tee ee swoy meel-YO-ree TEHR-mee-nee?

Certainly! We have offered you . . .
Certo! Le abbiamo offerta . . .
CHEHR-toh! leh ahb-B'YA-mo oh-FEHR-ta . . .

. . . our best dealers discount.
. . . il nostro migliore sconto per commercianti.
*. . . eel NOHS-tro meel-YO-reh SCOHN-toh pair ko-mair-
CHAHN-tee.*

Would you like to sign the contract now?
Desidera firmare adesso il contratto?
*deh-zee-DEH-ra feer-MA-reh ah-DESS-so eel cohn-
TRAHT-toh?*

We are in agreement, aren't we?
Siamo d'accordo, non è vero?
S'YA-mo dahk-COR-doh, nohn eh VEH-ro?

We need time to examine the contract.
Abbiamo bisogno di tempo per esaminare il contratto.
*ahb-B'YA-mo bee-SOHN-yo dee TEM-po pehr eh-sa-mee-
NA-reh eel cohn-TRAHT-toh.*

Our lawyers will be in contact with you.
I nostri avvocati si metteranno in contatto con Lei.
*ee NOHS-tree ahv-vo-CA-tee see met-teh-RAHN-no een
cohn-TAHT-toh cohn lay.*

It's a pleasure to do business with you.
È un piacere fare affari con Lei.
eh oon p'ya-CHEH-reh FA-reh ahf-FA-ree cohn lay.

We would like to invite you to dinner.
Vorremmo invitarLa a cena.
vor-REHM-mo een vee-TAR-la ah CHEH-na.

Can we call for you at eight o'clock?
Possiamo venire a prenderLa alle otto?
*pohs-S'YA-mo veh-NEE-reh ah pren-DEHR-la AHL-leh
  OHT-to?*

Thank you for the invitation.
Grazie per l'invito.
GRAHTS-yeh pair leen-VEE-toh.

. . . for the dinner.	**. . . for everything.**
. . . per la cena.	. . . per tutto.
. . . pair la CHEH-na.	*. . . pair TOOT-toh.*

It was a great pleasure . . .
È stato un grande piacere . . .
eh STA-toh oon GRAHN-deh p'ya-CHEH-reh . . .

. . . to meet you.
. . . co-nos-cer-LA.
. . . co-no-SHEHR-la.

When you plan . . .
Quando ha intenzione . . .
KWAHN-doh ah een-ten-T'SYO-neh . . .

. . . to visit America.
. . . di visitare l'America.
. . . de vee-zee-TA-reh la-MEH-ree-ka.

. . . please let me know in advance.
. . . La prego di farmelo sapere in anticipo.
*. . . la PREH-go dee FAR-meh-lo sa-PEH-reh een ahn-
  TEE-chee-po.*

We would like to return . . .
Vorremmo ricambiare . . .
vor-REHM-mo ree-cahm-B'YA-reh . . .

. . . your generous hospitality.
. . . la sua generosa ospitalità.
. . . la SOO-wa jen-neh-RO-za oh-spree-ta-lee-TA.

**25. Good News
(Una Buona Notizia)**

English and Italian share a great number of words. This is from the influence of Latin, the language of the Roman Empire, once spoken throughout the Christian world. In modern Italian these words are easy to recognize when one makes a slight spelling change, usually in the last syllable. They then become easy to understand and say, especially since you are already familiar with the Italian pronunciation as presented throughout this book.

Here are some of the English or Italian words according to their spelling changes.

English words ending in **-tion** are equivalent to Italian words ending in **-zione:**

condizione	revoluzione
immigrazione	interpretazione
identificazione	nazione
imitazione	emozione
conversazione	

and hundreds of others.

English words ending in **-ion** can become Italian simply by adding an "e":

unione
confusione
conclusione
fusione

The final **-al** and also **-ar** adds an "e":

fatale
animale
liberale
finale

populare
particulare

English words ending in **-ism** add an "o," as do words ending
in **-ment**:

optimismo
pessimismo
socialismo
capitalismo
documento
supplimento

The final **-ous** changes to **-oso** in Italian:

vigoroso
fabuloso
generoso

Many English words ending in **-it**, **-ite**, or **-ate** end in "o" in
Italian:

deposito
favorito
delicato

English words ending in **-ent** or **-ant** add an "e" in Italian:

permanente	residente
presidente	immigrante
ingrediente	intelligente
importante	

English words ending in **-ive** change the "e" to "o":

positivo
esecutivo
espansive
(N.B. Italian frequently uses "s" for "x.")

The English suffix -**ble** changes to -**bile**:

possibile
incredibile
probabile
responsabile

The suffix -**ty** frequently changes to -**tà**:

realità
posibilità
libertà
verità
incerità

The above list does not include the English nouns or adjectives with the appended "o" ending in Italian without other changes, which are easily recognized:

italiano
americano
romano
rapido
fantastico
modesto

26. A New Type of Dictionary

The following dictionary gives a list of English words with their translation into Italian to enable you to make up your own sentences in addition to those given in the phrase book. By using these words together with the following advice and short cuts, you will be able to make up hundreds of sentences by yourself. Only one Italian equivalent is given for each English word—the one most immediately useful to you—so that you won't be in any doubt about which word to use. Every word in the dictionary is followed by its phonetic pronunciation, so you will have no trouble being understood.

All Italian nouns are either masculine or feminine. If a noun ends in **-o**, it is usually masculine; if it ends in **-a**, it is usually feminine. The gender of any exceptions to this rule and of nouns ending in **-e** or any other letter is noted by an "(m)" or "(f)" after the noun in the dictionary.

Adjectives usually come after their nouns. All adjectives in this dictionary are given in the masculine form only. An adjective that ends in **-o** must change its ending to **-a** when it goes with a feminine noun:

> **il cappello nuovo** the new hat
> (**Il** is the masculine form for "the.")
> **la casa nuova** the new house
> (**La** is the feminine form for "the.")

Adjectives that end in **-e** are the same for both masculine and feminine:

> **il cappello grande**   the big hat
> **la casa grande**   the big house

(The word for "the" becomes **l'** before either masculine or feminine nouns beginning with a vowel: **l'uomo**—the man. And it becomes **lo** before masculine nouns beginning with **s** followed by another consonant or with **z: lo specchio**—the mirror.)

Nouns and adjectives that end in **-o** or **-e** form their plurals by changing the ending to **-i**. Those that end in **-a** form the plural by changing **-a** to **-e**:

> **i cappelli nuovi (grandi)** the new (big) hats
> (**I** is the masculine plural form for "the.")
> **le case nuove (grandi)** the new (big) houses
> (**Le** is the feminine plural form for "the.")

(The word for "the" becomes **gli** in the plural before masculine nouns beginning either with a vowel, with **s** followed by another consonant, or with **z: gli uomini**—the men; **gli specchi**—the mirrors.)

The verbs in the dictionary are given in the infinitive form. In actual use, their endings change according to the subject. Although a full grammatical explanation is not within the scope of this book, the following table will help you to use and recognize the present-tense forms of most of the verbs in the dictionary. These are very important because the subject pronouns—"I," "you," "he," "she," etc.—are frequently dropped and only the *ending* of the verb indicates the person referred to.

Verbs are divided into three groups according to their infinitive endings **-are, ere,** and **ire. Parlare** (to speak), **vendere** (to sell), and **partire** (to leave) are examples of the first, second, and third groups. Each verb has six forms in each tense, depending on what person or persons is referred to. Here is the present tense of **parlare** (to speak) with its English equivalents:

(io) parlo	I speak, I am speaking
(tu) parli	you (familiar) speak, you are speaking
(Lei, egli, ella) parla	you (formal) speak, you are speaking: he, she speaks; he, she is speaking
(noi) parliamo	we speak, we are speaking

(voi) parlate   you (plural) speak, you are
                                     speaking

(Loro, essi, esse) parlano   you (plural, formal), they (m
                                     or f) speak; you, they are
                                     speaking

The six forms for the present tense of **vendere** and **partire**
are:

vendo, vendi, vende, vendiamo, vendete, vendono
parto, parti, parte, partiamo, partite, partono.

There is another group of verbs ending in **-ire** which form
their present tense like **capire** (to understand):

capisco, capisci, capisce, capiamo, capite, capiscono

Many important verbs are somewhat irregular in their
forms. These appear in different sections of the phrase book
in the forms most useful for you to know and use. In addition,
in order to help you make your own sentences, the present
tense of "to be," "to go," "to come," "to have," and "to
want" are given within the dictionary.

We put the Italian pronouns above in parentheses to remind you that they are often dropped in conversation, as the
verb *ending* is what is important. We have not indicated a
pronoun for "it" because in Italian everything is masculine or
feminine and therefore "it" is "he" or "she."

Tu, Lei, voi, and **Loro** all mean "you." However *you*
should use the polite form **Lei** when speaking to one person
and **Loro** when speaking to more than one. The familiar
forms **tu** and **voi** are commonly used within the family, between close friends, among students, and to children.

You can do a lot of communicating by using simply the
present tense. But, in addition, you can use the infinitive to
express a variety of other concepts. To say something must
be done or is necessary, use **è necessario** directly with the
infinitive:

It is necessary to leave. **È necessario partire.**

To say you want to do something or to invite someone to do something, use the appropriate form of "to want" with the infinitive of the second verb:

> I want to go.   **Voglio andare.**
> Do you want to go?   **Vuole andare?**

For the negative, use **non** in front of the verb:

> I don't want to go.   **Non voglio andare.**

To give a polite command, add **-i** to the stem of the first conjugation, and **-a** for the other two:

> Speak!   **Parli!**
> Leave!   **Parta!**

For basic conversational purposes the present tense of "to go"—**andare**—can indicate the future according to the context: "Next year, we're going to Italy"—**L'anno prossimo, andiamo in Italia.**

Although the Italian present tense of verbs is equivalent to both the English simple present tense and the present progressive tense, you can also use the Italian present participle with the present tense form of **stare** (to be), exactly like the English progressive. The present participle ends in **-ando** for a verb whose infinitive ends in **-are**, and in **-endo** for a verb whose infinitive ends in **-ere** or **-ire**:

> I am eating.   **Sto mangiando.**

To form the conversational past or perfect tense, use the present tense of **avere** (to have) or **essere** (to be) with the past participle of the verb. The past participles of verbs of the first group end in **-ato;** those of the second group end in **-uto, -eso,** or **-esso;** and those of the third in **-ito**. Some important past participles that are formed irregularly are listed in the dictionary. Most verbs use **avere** to form the past tense:

> I gave, I have given   **ho dato**
> we received, we have   **abbiamo ricevuto**
>   received
> you finished, you have   **ha finito**
>   finished

Verbs that use "to be"—**essere**— to make the past tense are usually those of coming, going, arriving, leaving, etc.:

> I left, I have left   **Sono partito**
> the arrived, he has arrived   **È arrivato**

The past participle used with **essere** is like an adjective in that it agrees with the subject. A woman would say: **Sono partita**—I left.

Italian is fond of contractions: "To the"—**a** in combination with the definite article **il, lo, la, l', gli,** or **le**—becomes **al, allo, alla, all', ai, agli,** or **alle** respectively. "Of the"—**di** plus **il, lo, la, l', i, gli,** or **le**—becomes **del, dello, della, dell', dei, degli,** or **delle;** these forms are also used to mean "some" or "any."

The ubiquitous little words **ci** and **ne** take the place of the combinations of **a** and **di** respectively with another word when that word has already been referred to. **Ci** stands for the combination of **a** with the definite article and a noun and means "to it," "to them," or "there"; **ne** stands for the combination of **di** with the definite article and a noun and means "of it," "of them," "some," or "any":

> She's going there.   **Ci va.**
> I want two of them.   **Ne voglio due.**

The possessive of nouns is always expressed by **di:**

> Robert's house   **la casa di Roberto**

The possessive pronouns are listed individually in the dictionary. Observe that these pronouns agree in gender and number with the noun they refer to (not with the gender of the person possessing as in English):

| my hat and his (hers) | il mio cappello ed il suo |
| my house and his (hers) | la mia casa e la sua |

Object pronouns are given alphabetically within the dictionary. In sentences they are generally placed before the verb:

Tell me.	Mi dica.
Don't tell her anything.	Non le dica niente.
She gives him the check.	Ella gli da l'assegno.

With this advice and the indications given in the dictionary, you will be able to use this communicating dictionary to make up countless sentences on your own and to converse with anyone you may meet.

There is, of course, much more to Italian grammar than these few suggestions we have given you—for example, the other moods and tenses, irregularities of the Italian verb, the different types of pronouns, the diminutives of nouns, and the numerous idioms and sayings that reflect the wisdom, poetry, and history of Italian culture. But you can effectively use this selected basic vocabulary as an important step, or even springboard, to enter the wonderful world that is the Italian heritage and, by practice, absorb and constantly improve your command of this melodious and beautiful language.

A

a, an	un, uno (m)	*oon, OO-no, OO-na, oon*
	una (f)	
	un (m or f)	
absent	assente	*ahs-SEN-teh*
about (concerning)	ah proposito di	*a pro-PO-zee-toh dee*
above	sopra	*SO-pra*
(to) accept	accettare	*aht-chet-TA-reh*
accident	incidente	*een-chee-DEN-teh*
account	conto	*KOHN-toh*
across	attraverso	*aht-tra-VAIR-so*
act	atto	*AHT-toh*
actor	attore	*aht-TOH-reh*
actress	attrice	*aht-TREE-cheh*
address	indirizzo	*een-dee-REET-tso*
admission (price)	entrata	*een-TRA-ta*
advertisement	reclame(f)	*reh-KLA-meh*
advice	consiglio	*kohn-SEEL-yo*
(to be) afraid	aver paura	*ah-VAIR pa-OO-ra*
Africa	Africa	*AH-free-ka*
African	africano	*ah-free-KA-no*
after	dopo	*DOH-po*
afternoon	pomeriggio	*po-meh-REED-jo*
again	ancora	*ahn-KO-ra*
against	contro	*KOHN-tro*
age	età	*eh-TA*
agency	agenzia	*ah-jent-SEE-ya*

157

agent	agente (m)	*ah-JEN-teh*
ago	fa	*fa*

(See page 26 for use.)

(to) agree	essere d'accordo	*ES-seh-reh dah-KOR-do*
ahead	avanti	*ah-VAHN-tee*
air	aria	*AHR-ya*
air conditioned	aria condizionata	*AHR-ya kohn-deets-yo-NA-ta*
air force	aeronautica	*ah-eh-ro-NOW-tee-ka*
(by) air mail	via aerea	*VEE-ah ah-EH-reh-ah*
airplane	aereo	*ah-EH-reh-oh*
airport	aereoporto	*ah-eh-reh-oh-POR-toh*
all	tutto	*TOOT-toh*
That's all!	È tutto!	*eh TOOT-toh!*
allow	permettere	*pair-MET-teh-reh*
all right	va bene	*va BEH-neh*
almost	quasi	*KWA-zee*
alone	solo	*SO-lo*
already	già	*ja*
also	anche	*AHN-keh*
always	sempre	*SEM-preh*
(I) am	sono	*SO-no*
	sto	*sto*

("*sto*" is used with the present participle. See page 154.)

America	America	*ah-MEH-ree-ka*
American	americano	*ah-meh-ree-KA-no*
amusing	divertente	*dee-vehr-TEN-teh*
and	e, ed (before a vowel)	*eh, ed*
angry	arrabbiato	*ar-rahb-B'YA-toh*
animal	animale (m)	*ah-nee-MA-leh*
ankle	caviglia	*ka-VEEL-ya*
annoying	noioso	*no-YO-so*
another	un altro	*oon AHL-tro*
answer	risposta	*rees-PO-sta*
antiseptic	antisettico	*ahn-tee-SET-tee-ko*
any	ne	*neh*

(See introduction to the dictionary.)

anyone	qualsiasi persona	*kwahl-SEE-ah-see pair-SO-na*
anything	qualsiasi cosa	*kwahl-SEE-ah-see KO-za*
anywhere	qualsiasi posto	*kwahl-SEE-ah-see PO-sto*
apartment	apartamento	*ahp-par-ta-MEN-toh*
apple	mela	*MEH-la*
appointment	appuntamento	*ahp-poon-ta-MEN-toh*
April	aprile	*ah-PREE-leh*
Arab, Arabic	arabo	*AH-ra-bo*
architecture	architettura	*ar-kee-tet-TOO-ra*
are		
you (sg) are	Lei è	*lay eh*

we are	siamo	S'YA-mo
you (pl) are	Loro sono	LO-ro SO-no
they are	sono	SO-no
there are	ci sono	chee SO-no

(The following forms are used with the present participle. See introduction to the dictionary.)

you (sg) are	Lei sta	lay sta
we are	stiamo	STYA-mo
you (pl) are	Loro stanno	LO-ro STAHN-no
they are	stanno	STAHN-no
arm	braccio	BRAHT-cho
army	esercito	eh-ZAIR-chee-toh
around (surrounding)	intorno	een-TOR-no
around (approximately)	circa	CHEER-ka
(to) arrive	arrivare	ar-ree-VA-reh
art	arte (f)	AR-teh
artist	artista (m)	ar-TEES-ta
as	come	KO-meh
Asia	Asia	AHS-ya
(to) ask	domandare	doh-mahn-DA-reh
asleep	addormentato	ahd-dor-men-TA-toh
asparagus	asparagi (m pl)	ahs-PA-ra-jee
aspirin	aspirina	ahs-pee-REE-na
ass	asino	AH-see-no
at (location)	a, in	ah, een

at (time)	alle	*AHL-leh*
Atlantic	Atlantico	*aht-LAHN-tee-ko*
atomic	atomico	*ah-TOH-mee-ko*
August	agosto	*ah-GOHS-toh*
aunt	zia	*DZEE-ah*
Australia	Australia	*ows-TRAHL-ya*
Australian	australiano	*ows-trahl-YA-no*
Austria	Austria	*OWS-tr'ya*
Austrian	austriaco	*ows-TREE-ah-ko*
author	autore (m)	*ow-TOH-reh*
automatic	automatico	*ow-toh-MA-tee-ko*
automobile	automobile (f)	*ow-toh-MO-bee-leh*
autumn	autunno	*ow-TOON-no*
(to) avoid	evitare	*eh-vee-TA-reh*
away	via	*VEE-ah*

B

baby	bebè (m)	*beh-BEH*
bachelor	scapolo	*SKA-po-lo*
back (part of body)	schiena	*SK'YEH-na*
bad	cattivo	*kaht-TEE-vo*
baggage	bagaglio	*ba-GAHL-yo*
balcony (theater)	balconata	*bahl-ko-NA-ta*
banana	banana	*ba-NA-na*

bandage	benda	*BEN-da*
bank	banca	*BAHN-ka*
bar	bar	*bar*
barber	barbiere (m)	*bar-B'YEH-reh*
baritone	baritono	*ba-REE-toh-no*
basso	basso	*BAHS-so*
bath	bagno	*BAHN-yo*
bathing suit	costume da bagno	*kohs-TOO-meh da BAHN-yo*
bathroom	stanza da bango	*STAHNT-sa da BAHN-yo*
battery	batteria	*baht-teh-REE-ya*
battle	battaglia	*baht-TAHL-ya*
(to) be	essere	*EHS-seh-reh*

(See also "am," "is," "are," "was," "were," "been.")

beach	spiaggia	*SP'YAHD-ja*
beans	fagioli (m pl)	*fa-JO-lee*
beard	barba	*BAR-ba*
beautiful	bello	*BEL-lo*
beauty	bellezza	*bel-LET-tsa*
beauty shop	salone di bellezza	*sa-LO-neh dee bel-LET-tsa*
because	perchè	*pair-KEH*
bed	letto	*LET-toh*
bedroom	stanza da letto	*STAHNT-sa da LET-toh*
beef	manzo	*MAHNT-so*

been	stato	*STA-toh*
beer	birra	*BEER-ra*
before	prima	*PREE-ma*
(to) begin	cominciare	*ko-meen-CHA-reh*
behind	dietro	*D'YEH-tro*
(to) believe	credere	*KREH-deh-reh*
belt	cintura	*cheen-TOO-ra*
beside	vicino a	*vee-CHEE-no ah*
best (adj)	il migliore	*eel meel-YO-reh*
better	meglio	*MAIL-yo*
between	tra	*tra*
bicycle	bicicletta	*bee-chee-CLET-ta*
big	grande	*GRAHN-deh*
bill	conto	*KOHN-toh*
bird	uccello	*oot-CHEL-lo*
birthday	compleanno	*kohm-pleh-AHN-no*
black	nero	*NEH-ro*
blond	biondo	*B'YOHN-doh*
blood	sangue (m)	*SAHN-gweh*
blouse	blusa	*BLOO-za*
blue	blu	*bloo*
boardinghouse	pensione	*pens-YO-neh*
boat	barca	*BAR-ka*
body	corpo	*KOR-po*
book	libro	*LEE-bro*
bookstore	libreria	*lee-breh-REE-ya*

born	nato	*NA-toh*
(to) borrow	imprestare	*eem-pres-TA-reh*
boss	padrone (m)	*pa-DRO-neh*
both	entrambi	*en-TRAHM-bee*
(to) bother	disturbare	*dees-toor-BA-reh*
bottle	bottiglia	*boht-TEEL-ya*
bottom	fondo	*FOHN-doh*
bought	comprato	*kohm-PRA-toh*
box (carton)	scatola	*SKA-toh-la*
box (theater)	palco	*PAHL-ko*
boy	ragazzo	*ra-GAHT-tso*
brain	cervello	*chair-VEL-lo*
brake	freno	*FREH-no*
brave	coraggioso	*ko-rahd-JO-so*
bread	pane (m)	*PA-neh*
(to) break	rompere	*ROHM-peh-reh*
breakfast	colazione (f)	*ko-lahts-YO-neh*
(to) breathe	respirare	*res-pee-RA-reh*
bridge	ponte (m)	*POHN-teh*
briefcase	cartella	*kar-TEL-la*
(to) bring	portare	*por-TA-reh*
Bring me . . .	Mi porti . . .	*mee POR-tee*
broken	rotto	*ROHT-toh*
brother	fratello	*fra-TEL-lo*
brother-in-law	cognato	*kohn-YA-toh*
brown	marrone	*mar-RO-neh*
brunette	bruna	*BROO-na*

(to) build	costruire	*kohs-troo-EE-reh*
building	edificio	*eh-dee-FEE-cho*
built	costruito	*kohs-troo-EE-toh*
bureau	burò	*boo-RO*
bus	autobus (m)	*OW-toh-booss*
business	affari (m pl)	*ahf-FA-ree*
business trip	viaggio d'affari	*V'YAHD-jo dahf-FA-ree*
bus stop	fermata dell'autobus	*fair-MA-ta del-L'OW-toh-booss*
busy	occupato	*ohk-koo-PA-toh*
but	ma	*ma*
butter	burro	*BOOR-ro*
button	buttone (m)	*boht-TOH-neh*
(to) buy	comprare	*kohm-PRA-reh*
by	per	*pair*

C

cabbage	cavolo	*KA-vo-lo*
cake	torta (f)	*TOR-ta*
(to) call	chiamare	*k'ya-MA-reh*
Call me.	Mi chiami.	*mee K'YA-mee.*
camera	macchina fotografica	*MAHK-kee-na fo-toh-GRA-fee ka*
can (to be able)	potere	*po-TEH-reh*
Can you . . . ?	Può Lei . . . ?	*pwo lay . . . ?*

I can	posso	*POHS-so*
I can't	non posso	*nohn POHS-so*
can (container)	scatola di latta	*SKA-toh-la-dee LAHT-ta*
canal	canale (m)	*ka-NA-leh*
candy	caramella (f)	*ka-ra-MEL-la*
can opener	apriscatole (m)	*ah-pree-SKA-toh-leh*
capable	capace	*ka-PA-cheh*
captain	capitano	*ka-pee-TA-no*
car	macchina	*MAHK-kee-na*
carburetor	carburatore (m)	*kar-boo-ra-TOH-reh*
card	carta	*KAR-ta*
careful	attento	*aht-TEN-toh*
(Be) careful!	Attenzione!	*aht-tents-YO-neh!*
careless	disattento	*dees-aht-TEN-toh*
carrot	carota	*ka-RO-ta*
(to) carry	portare	*por-TA-reh*
Carry this to . . .	Porti questo a . . .	*POR-tee KWES-toh ah . . .*
cashier	cassiere (m)	*kahs-S'YEH-reh*
castle	castello	*kahs-TEL-lo*
cat	gatto	*GAHT-toh*
cathedral	cattedrale (f)	*kaht-teh-DRA-leh*
Catholic	cattolico	*kaht-TOH-lee-ko*
celebration	celebrazione (f)	*cheh-leh-brahts-YO-neh*

cellar	cantina	*kahn-TEE-na*
cemetery	cimetero	*chee-meh-TEH-ro*
cent	centesimo	*chen-TEH-see-mo*
center	centro	*CHEN-tro*
century	secolo	*SEH-ko-lo*
certainly	certamente	*chair-ta-MEN-teh*
certificate of origin	certificato d'origine	*chair-tee-fee-KA-toh doh-REE-jee-neh*
chair	sedia	*SAY-d'ya*
change	cambiamento	*kahm-b'ya-MEN-toh*
(to) change	cambiare	*kahm-B'YA-reh*
charming	affascinante	*ahf-fah-shee-NAHN-teh*
chauffeur	autista (m)	*ow-TEES-ta*
cheap	a buon mercato	*ah bwohn mair-KA-toh*
check	assegno	*ahs-SEN-yo*
checkroom	guardaroba	*gwar-da-RO-ba*
cheese	formaggio	*for-MAHD-jo*
cherries	ciliege (f pl)	*cheel-YEH-jeh*
chest	petto	*PET-toh*
chicken	pollo	*POHL-lo*
child	bambino	*bahm-BEE-no*
chin	mento	*MEN-toh*
China	Cina	*CHEE-na*
Chinese	cinese	*chee-NEH-zeh*
chocolate	cioccolata	*chohk-ko-LA-ta*

chop	costoletta	*kohs-toh-LET-ta*
church	chiesa	*K'YEH-za*
cigar	sigaro	*SEE-ga-ro*
cigarette	sigaretta	*see-ga-RET-ta*
city	città	*cheet-TA*
(to) clean	pulire	*poo-LEE-reh*
clear	chiaro	*K'YA-ro*
clever	intelligente	*een-tel-lee-JEN-teh*
climate	clima	*KLEE-ma*
close (near)	vicino	*vee-CHEE-no*
(to) close	chiudere	*K'YOO-deh-reh*
closed	chiuso	*K'YOO-zo*
clothes	vestiti (m pl)	*ves-TEE-tee*
coast	costa	*KOHS-ta*
coat	cappotto	*kahp-POHT-toh*
coffee	caffè (m)	*kahf-FEH*
coin	moneta	*mo-NEH-ta*
cold	freddo	*FRED-doh*
college	università	*oon-nee-vair-see-TA*
colonel	colonnello	*ko-lohn-NEL-lo*
color	colore (m)	*ko-LO-reh*
comb	pettine (m)	*PET-tee-neh*
(to) come	venire	*veh-NEE-reh*
I come	vengo	*VEN-go*
you (sg) **come**	Lei viene	*lay V'YEH-neh*
he, she comes	viene	*V'YEH-neh*
we come	veniamo	*ven-YA-mo*

you (pl) come	Loro vengono	*LO-ro VEN-go-no*
they come	vengono	*VEN-go-no*
Come!	Venga!	*VEN-ga!*
Come in!	Avanti!	*ah-VAHN-tee!*
(to) come back	ritornare	*ree-tor-NA-reh*
company	compagnia	*kohm-pahn-YEE-ah*
competition	competizione (f)	*kohm-peh-teets-YO-neh*
complete	completo	*kohm-PLEH-toh*
computer	calcolatore (m)	*kahl-ko-la-TOH-reh*
concert	concerto	*kohn-CHAIR-toh*
conductor	conduttore (m)	*kohn-doot-TOH-reh*
congratulations	congratulazioni (f pl)	*kohn-gra-too-lahts-YO-nee*
(to) continue	continuare	*kohn-tee-NWA-reh*
conversation	conversazione (f)	*kohn-vair-sahts-YO-neh*
cook	cuoco (m), cuoca (f)	*KOW-ko, KWO-ka*
(to) cook	cucinare	*koo-chee-NA-reh*
cool	fresco	*FRES-ko*
copy	copia	*KOHP-ya*
corkscrew	cavatappi (m)	*ka-va-TAHP-pee*
corner	angolo	*AHN-go-lo*
correct	esatto	*eh-ZAHT-toh*

(to) cost	costare	*kohs-TA-reh*
cotton	cotone (m)	*ko-TOH-neh*
cough	tosse (f)	*TOS-seh*
country	paese (m)	*pa-EH-zeh*
cousin	cugino	*koo-JEE-no*
cow	mucca	*MOOK-ka*
crab	granchio	*GRAHNK-yo*
crazy	matto	*MAHT-toh*
(to) crate	imballare	*eem-bahl-LA-reh*
cream	crema	*KREH-ma*
(to) cross	incrociare	*een-kro-CHA-reh*
crossing	incrocio	*een-KRO-cho*
cup	tazza	*TAHT-tsa*
custom (habit)	usanza	*oo-SAHNT-sa*
customs form	formulario di dogana	*for-moo-LAR-yo dee doh-GA-na*
customs office	ufficio di dogana	*oof-FEE-cho dee doh-GA-na*
(to) cut	tagliare	*tahl-YA-reh*

D

(to) dance	ballare	*bahl-LA-reh*
dangerous	pericoloso	*peh-ree-ko-LO-zo*
dark	scuro	*SKOO-ro*
darling	tesoro	*teh-ZO-ro*

date (day)	data	*DA-ta*
date (appointment)	appuntamento	*ahp-poon-ta-MEN-toh*
daughter	figlia	*FEEL-ya*
daughter-in-law	nuora	*NWO-ra*
day	giorno	*JOR-no*
dead	morto	*MOR-toh*
dear	caro	*KA-ro*
December	dicembre	*dee-CHEM-breh*
(to) decide	decidere	*deh-CHEE-deh-reh*
deep	profondo	*pro-FOHN-doh*
delay	ritardo	*ree-TAR-doh*
delicious	delizioso	*deh-leets-YO-zo*
delighted	contento	*kohn-TEN-toh*
dentist	dentista (m)	*den-TEES-ta*
department store	grande magazzino	*GRAHN-deh ma-gahd-DZEE-no*
desk	scrivania	*skree-va-NEE-ya*
detour	deviazione (f)	*dev-yahts-YO-neh*
devil	diavolo	*D'YA-vo-lo*
dictionary	dizionario	*deets-yo-NAHR-yo*
different	differente	*deef-feh-REN-teh*
difficult	difficile	*deef-FEE-chee-leh*
(to) dine	pranzare	*prahnt-SA-reh*
dining room	sala da pranzo	*SA-la da PRAHNT-so*
dinner	pranzo	*PRAHNT-so*

direction	direzione (f)	*dee-rets-YO-neh*
dirty	sporco	*SPOR-ko*
disappointed	dispiaciuto	*dees-p'ya-CHOO-toh*
discount	sconto	*SKOHN-toh*
divorced	divorziato	*dee-vorts-YA-toh*
(to) do	fare	*FA-reh*

"Do" is not used to ask a question or to form the negative. For a question, simply put the subject after the verb; and for the negative, use **non** before the verb:

Do you want . . . ?	Vuole Lei . . . ?	*VWO-leh lay . . . ?*
I don't understand.	Non capisco.	*nohn ka-PEES-ko.*
Don't do that!	Non faccia così!	*nohn FAHT-cha ko-ZEE!*
dock	molo	*MO-lo*
doctor	dottore (m)	*doht-TOH-reh*
dog	cane (m)	*Ka-neh*
dollar	dollaro	*DOHL-la-ro*
door	porta	*POR-ta*
down	giù	*joo*
downtown	al centro	*ahl CHEN-tro*
dress	vestito	*ves-TEE-toh*
(to) drink	bere	*BEH-reh*
(to) drive	guidare	*gwee-DA-reh*
driver	autista (m)	*ow-TEES-ta*
driver's license	patente (f)	*pa-TEN-teh*

drugstore	farmacia	*far-ma-CHEE-ya*
drunk	ubriaco	*oo-bree-AH-ko*
dry cleaner	pulitore a secco (m)	*poo-lee-TOH-reh ah SEK-ko*
duck	anitra	*AH-nee-tra*

E

each	ognuno	*ohn-YOO-no*
ear	orecchio	*oh-REK-k'yo*
early	presto	*PRES-toh*
(to) earn	guadagnare	*gwa-dahn-YA-reh*
earth	terra	*TAIR-ra*
east	est (m)	*est*
easy	facile	*FA-chee-leh*
(to) eat	mangiare	*mahn-JA-reh*
eggs	uova (f pl)	*WO-va*
eight	otto	*OHT-toh*
eighteen	diciotto	*dee-CHOHT-toh*
eighty	ottanta	*oht-TAHN-ta*
either (one)	l'uno o l'altro	*LOO-no oh LAHL-tro*
either . . . or	o . . . o	*oh . . . oh*
elbow	gomito	*GO-mee-toh*
electric	elettrico	*eh-LET-tree-ko*
elephant	elefante (m)	*eh-leh-FAHN-teh*
elevator	ascensore (m)	*ah-shen-SO-reh*

embassy	ambasciata	*ahm-ba-SHA-ta*
emergency	emergenza	*eh-mair-JENT-sa*
(to) employ	impiegare	*eem-p'yeh-GA-reh*
employee	impiegato	*eem-p'yeh-GA-toh*
end	fine (f)	*FEE-neh*
(to) end	finire	*fee-NEE-reh*
England	Inghilterra	*een-gheel-TAIR-ra*
English	inglese	*een-GLEH-zeh*
entertaining	divertente	*dee-vair-TEN-teh*
error	errore (m)	*air-RO-reh*
especially	specialmente	*speh-chahl-MEN-teh*
Europe	Europa	*eh-oo-RO-pa*
European	europeo	*eh-oo-ro-PEH-oh*
even	perfino	*pair-FEE-no*
evening	sera	*SEH-ra*
ever (sometime)	mai	*my*
every	ogni	*OHN-yee*
everybody	tutti	*TOOT-tee*
everything	tutto	*TOOT-toh*
exactly	esattamente	*eh-zaht-ta-MEN-teh*
excellent	eccellente	*et-chel-LEN-teh*
except	eccetto	*et-CHET-toh*
(to) exchange	cambiare	*kahm-B'YA-reh*
Excuse me!	Mi scusi!	*mee SKOO-zee!*
exit	uscita	*oo-SHEE-ta*
expensive	costoso	*ko-STO-zo*

experience	esperienza	*es-pair-YENT-sa*
explanation	spiegazione (f)	*sp'yeh-gahts-YO-neh*
(to) export	esportare	*es-por-TA-reh*
extra	extra	*EX-tra*
eye	occhio	*OHK-k'yo*

F

face	faccia	*FAHT-cha*
fair (exposition)	fiera	*FYEH-ra*
factory	fabbrica	*FAHB-bree-ka*
fall (autumn)	autunno	*ow-TOON-no*
(to) fall	cadere	*ka-DEH-reh*
family	famiglia	*fa-MEEL-ya*
famous	famoso	*fa-MO-zo*
far	lontano	*lohn-TA-no*
How far?	Quanto è lontano?	*KWAHN-toh eh lohn-TA-no?*
farm	fattoria	*faht-toh-REE-ya*
farther	più lontano	*p'yoo lohn-TA-no*
fast	veloce	*veh-LO-cheh*
fat	grasso	*GRAHS-so*
father	padre (m)	*PA-dreh*
February	febbraio	*feb-BRA-yo*
(to) feel	sentire	*sen-TEE-reh*
fever	febbre (f)	*FEB-breh*

few	pochi	*PO-kee*
fifteen	quindici	*KWEEN-dee-chee*
fifty	cinquanta	*cheen-KWAHN-ta*
(to) fight	combattere	*kohm-BAHT-teh-reh*
(to) fill	riempire	*r'yem-PEE-reh*
film (movie)	film (m)	*feelm*
film (for camera)	pellicola	*pel-LEE-ko-la*
finally	finalmente	*fee-nahl-MEN-teh*
(to) find	trovare	*tro-VA-reh*
(to) find out	scoprire	*sko-PREE-reh*
finger	dito	*DEE-toh*
(to) finish	finire	*fee-NEE-reh*
finished	finito	*fee-NEE-toh*
fire	fuoco	*FWO-ko*
first	primo	*PREE-mo*
fish	pesce (m)	*PEH-sheh*
(to) fish	pescare	*pess-KA-reh*
five	cinque	*CHEEN-kweh*
flight	volo	*VO-lo*
floor	pavimento	*pa-vee-MEN-toh*
flower	fiore (m)	*F'YO-reh*
fly (insect)	mosca	*MO-ska*
(to) fly	volare	*vo-LA-reh*
food	cibo	*CHEE-bo*
foot	piede (m)	*P'YEH-deh*
for	per	*pair*

foreigner	straniero	*strahn-YEH-ro*
forest	foresta	*fo-RESS-ta*
(to) forget	dimenticare	*dee-men-tee-KA-reh*
Don't forget!	Non si dimentichi!	*nohn see dee-MEN-tee-kee!*
fork	forchetta	*for-KET-ta*
forty	quaranta	*kwa-RAHN-ta*
fountain	fontana	*fohn-TA-na*
four	quattro	*KWAHT-tro*
fourteen	quattordici	*kwaht-TOR-dee-chee*
fox	volpe (f)	*VOHL-peh*
France	Francia	*FRAHN-cha*
free	libero	*LEE-beh-ro*
French	francese	*frahn-CHEH-zeh*
frequently	frequentemente	*freh-kwen-teh-MEN-teh*
fresh	fresco	*FRESS-ko*
Friday	venerdì	*ven-air-DEE*
fried	fritto	*FREET-toh*
friend	amico	*ah-MEE-ko*
frog	rana	*RA-na*
from	da	*da*
(in) front of	davanti a	*da-VAHN-tee ah*
fruit	frutto	*FROOT-toh*
full	pieno	*P'YEH-no*
funny	buffo	*BOOF-fo*
furniture	mobili (m pl)	*MO-bee-lee*

| **future** | futuro | *foo-TOO-ro* |
| in the future | nel futuro | *nel foo-TOO-ro* |

G

game	gioco	*JO-ko*
garage	garage (m)	*ga-RAHZH*
garden	giardino	*jar-DEE-no*
gas	gas (m)	*gahss*
gas station	stazione di benzina (f)	*stahts-YO-neh dee bend-ZEE-na*
general (n or adj)	generale	*jen-eh-RA-leh*
gentleman	signore (m)	*seen-YO-reh*
German	tedesco	*teh-DESS-ko*
Germany	Germania	*jer-MAHN-ya*
(to) get (obtain)	ottenere	*oht-teh-NEH-reh*
(to) get (become)	diventare	*dee-ven-TA-reh*
(to) get off	scendere	*SHEN-deh-reh*
(to) get on	salire	*sa-LEE-reh*
(to) get out	uscire	*oo-SHEE-reh*
Get out!	Esca!	*ESS-ka!*
gift	regalo	*reh-GA-lo*
(to) give	dare	*DA-reh*
Give me . . .	Mi dia . . .	*mee DEE-ya . . .*
girl	ragazza	*ra-GAHT-tsa*
glass (for drinking)	bicchiere (m)	*beek-K'YEH-reh*

glass (for windows)	vetro	*VEH-tro*
(eye) glasses	occhiali (m pl)	*ohk-K'ya-lee*
glove	guanto	*GWAHN-toh*
(to) go	andare	*ahn-DA-reh*
I go	vado	*VA-doh*
You (sg) **go**	Lei va	*lay va*
he, she goes	va	*va*
we go	andiamo	*ahnd-YA-mo*
you (pl) **go**	Loro vanno	*LO-ro VAHN-no*
they go	vanno	*VAHN-no*
(to) go away	andare via	*ahn-DA-reh VEE-ya*
Go away!	Vada via!	*VA-da VEE-ya!*
(to) go back	ritornare	*ree-tor-NA-reh*
Go on!	Avanti!	*ah-VAHN-tee!*
goat	capra	*KA-pra*
God	Dio	*DEE-yo*
gold	oro	*OH-ro*
golf	golf (m)	*gohlf*
good	buono	*BWO-no*
Goodbye (formal)	ArrivederLa	*ahr-ree-veh-DAIR-la*
(less formal)	Arrivederci	*ahr-ree-veh-DAIR-chee*
(informal)	Ciao	*chow*
government	governo	*go-VAIR-no*
grandfather	nonno	*NOHN-no*
grandmother	nonna	*NOHN-na*
grapes	uva	*OO-va*

grateful	grato	*GRA-toh*
gray	grigio	*GREE-jo*
great	grande	*GRAHN-deh*
a great many	molti	*MOHL-tee*
Greece	Grecia	*GREH-cha*
Greek	greco	*GREH-ko*
green	verde	*VAIR-deh*
group	gruppo	*GROOP-po*
guide	guida	*GWEE-da*
guitar	chitarra	*kee-TAR-ra*

H

hair (m pl)	capelli	*ka-PEL-lee*
hairbrush	spazzola	*SPAHT-tso-la*
haircut	taglio di capelli	*TAHL-yo dee ka-PEL-lee*
half	metà	*meh-TA*
hand	mano (f)	*MA-no*
happy	felice	*feh-LEE-cheh*
hard	duro	*DOO-ro*
hat	cappello	*kahp-PEL-lo*
(to) have	avere	*ah-VEH-reh*
I have	ho	*oh*
you (sg) have	Lei ha	*lay ah*
he, she has	ha	*ah*
we have	abbiamo	*ahb-B'YA-mo*

you (pl) **have**	Loro hanno	*LO-ro AHN-no*
they have	hanno	*AHN-no*
Have you?	Ha?	*ah?*
he	egli, lui	*EL-yee, LOO-ee*
head	testa	*TESS-ta*
(to) hear	sentire	*sen-TEE-reh*
heart	cuore (m)	*KWO-reh*
heavy	pesante	*peh-ZAHN-teh*
Hello!	Ciao!	*chow!*
(on the telephone)	Pronto!	*PROHN-toh!*
(to) help	aiutare	*ah-yoo-TA-reh*
Help!	Aiuto!	*ah-YOO-toh!*
her (pronoun)	la, le, lei	*la, leh, lay*
her (adj)	il suo, la sua, (pl) i suoi, le sue	*eel SOO-wo, la SOO-wa, ee swoy, leh SOO-eh*
here	qui	*kwee*
high	alto	*AHL-toh*
highway	autostrada	*ow-toh-STRA-da*
hill	collina	*kohl-LEE-na*
him	lo, gli, lui	*lo, l'yee, LOO-ee*
his	il suo, la sua, (pl) i suoi, le sue	*eel SOO-wo, la SOO-wa, ee swoy, leh SOO-eh*
history	storia	*STOR-ya*
home	casa	*KA-za*

at home	a casa	*ah KA-za*
horse	cavallo	*ka-VAHL-lo*
on horseback	a cavallo	*ah ka-VAHL-lo*
hospital	ospedale (m)	*ohs-peh-DA-leh*
hot	caldo	*KAHL-doh*
hotel	albergo	*ahl-BAIR-go*
hour	ora	*OH-ra*
house	casa	*KA-za*
how	come	*KO-meh*
however	in ogni caso	*een OHN-yee KA-zo*
hundred	cento	*CHEN-toh*
a hundred and one	centouno	*chen-toh-OO-no*
Hungary	Ungheria	*oon-geh-REE-ya*
Hungarian	ungherese	*oon-geh-REH-zeh*
(to be) hungry	aver fame	*ah-VAIR FA-meh*
(to) hunt	cacciare	*kaht-CHA-reh*
(to) hurry	sbrigarsi	*zbree-GAR-see*
Hurry up!	Presto!	*PRESS-toh!*
husband	marito	*ma-REE-toh*

I

| I | io | *EE-yo* |
| ice | ghiaccio | *G'YAHT-cho* |

ice cream	gelato	*jeh-LA-toh*
idiot	idiota	*eed-YO-ta*
if	se	*seh*
ill	ammalato	*ahm-ma-LA-toh*
(to) import	importare	*eem-por-TA-reh*
important	importante	*eem-por-TAHN-teh*
impossible	impossibile	*eem-pohs-SEE-bee-leh*
in	in	*een*
included	incluso	*een-KLOO-zo*
industry	industria	*een-DOOS-tr'ya*
information	informazione (f)	*een-for-mahts-YO-neh*
inhabitant	abitante (m)	*ah-bee-TAHN-teh*
inside	dentro	*DEN-tro*
instead	invece	*een-VEH-cheh*
intelligent	intelligente	*een-tel-lee-JEN-teh*
interested	interessato	*een-teh-res-SA-toh*
interesting	interessante	*een-teh-res-SAHN-teh*
interpreter	interprete (m)	*een-TAIR-preh-teh*
into	in	*een*
(to) introduce	presentare	*preh-zen-TA-reh*
invitation	invito	*een-VEE-toh*
is	è	*eh*

is	sta	*sta*

(Used with the present participle. See introduction to the dictionary.)

island	isola	*EE-zo-la*
Israel	Israele	*eez-ra-EH-leh*
Israeli	israeliano	*eez-ra-el-YA-no*
it (object)	lo, la	*lo, la*
its	il suo, la sua	*eel SOO-wo, la SOO-wa*
Italian	italiano	*ee-tahl-YA-no*
Italy	Italia	*ee-TAHL-ya*

J

jacket	giacca	*JAHK-ka*
jail	prigione (f)	*pree-JO-neh*
January	gennaio	*jen-NA-yo*
Japan	Giappone	*jahp-PO-neh*
Japanese	giapponese	*jahp-po-NEH-zeh*
jewelry	gioielli (m pl)	*joy-YEL-lee*
Jewish	ebreo	*eh-BREH-oh*
job	lavoro	*la-VO-ro*
joke	scherzo	*SKAIRT-so*
July	luglio	*LOOL-yo*
June	giugno	*JOON-yo*
just (only)	soltanto	*sohl-TAHN-toh*
just now	proprio adesso	*PROHP-r'yo ah-DESS-so*

K

(to) keep	tenere	*teh-NEH-reh*
Keep out!	Fuori!	*FWO-ree!*
Keep quiet!	Silenzio!	*see-LENTS-yo!*
key	chiave (f)	*K'YA-veh*
kind (nice)	gentile	*jen-TEE-leh*
kind (type)	genere	*JEH-neh-reh*
king	re (m)	*reh*
kiss	bacio	*BA-cho*
kitchen	cucina	*koo-CHEE-na*
knee	ginocchio	*jee-NOHK-k'yo*
knife	coltello	*kohl-TEL-lo*
(to) know (a person)	conoscere	*ko-NO-sheh-reh*
(to) know (something)	sapere	*sa-PEH-reh*
Do you know . . . ?	Sa Lei . . . ?	*sa lay . . . ?*
Who knows?	Chi sa?	*kee sa?*

L

ladies' room	toeletta	*toh-eh-LET-ta*
lady	signora	*seen-YO-ra*
lake	lago	*LA-go*
lamb	agnello	*ahn-YEL-lo*

land	terra	*TAIR-ra*
language	lingua	*LEEN-gwa*
large	grande	*GRAHN-deh*
last	ultimo	*OOL-tee-mo*
late	tardi	*TAR-dee*
later	più tardi	*p'yoo TAR-dee*
law	legge (f)	*LED-jeh*
lawyer	avvocato	*ahv-vo-KA-toh*
(to) learn	imparare	*eem-pa-RA-reh*
leather	cuoio	*KWO-yo*
(to) leave (something)	lasciare	*la-SHA-reh*
(to) leave (depart)	partire	*par-TEE-reh*
left	sinistro	*see-NEE-stro*
leg	gamba	*GAHM-ba*
lemon	limone (m)	*lee-MO-neh*
(to) lend	prestare	*press-TA-reh*
less (adv)	meno	*MEH-no*
lesson	lezione (f)	*lets-YO-neh*
Let's go!	Andiamo!	*ahnd-YA-mo!*
letter	lettera	*LET-teh-ra*
lettuce	lattuga	*laht-TOO-ga*
liberty	libertà	*lee-bair-TA*
lieutenant	luogotenente (m)	*lwo-go-teh-NEN-teh*
life	vita	*VEE-ta*
light (weight)	leggero	*led-JEH-ro*
light (illumination)	luce (f)	*LOO-cheh*

like (prep)	come	*KO-meh*
Like this.	Così.	*ko-ZEE.*
(to) like	piacere	*p'ya-CHEH-reh*
linen	lino	*LEE-no*
lion	leone (m)	*leh-OH-neh*
lips	labbra (f pl)	*LAHB-bra*
liquor	liquore	*lee-KWOH-reh*
list	lista	*LEE-sta*
(to) listen	ascoltare	*ahs-kohl-TA-reh*
Listen!	Ascolti!	*ahs-KOHL-tee!*
little (small)	piccolo	*PEEK-ko-lo*
a little (of)	un poco (di)	*oon PO-ko (dee)*
(to) live	vivere	*VEE-veh-reh*
lived	vissuto	*vees-SOO-toh*
living room	salotto	*sa-LOHT-toh*
lobster	aragosta	*ah-ra-GO-sta*
long	lungo	*LOON-go*
(to) look	guardare	*gwahr-DA-reh*
Look!	Guardi!	*GWAHR-dee!*
Look out!	Attenti!	*aht-TEN-tee!*
loose	sciolto	*SHOHL-toh*
(to) lose	perdere	*PAIR-deh-reh*
loss	perdita	*PAIR-dee-ta*
lost	perduto	*pair-DOO-toh*
lot (much)	molto	*MOHL-toh*
(to) love	amare	*ah-MA-reh*
low	basso	*BAHS-so*

luck	fortuna	*for-TOO-na*
Good luck!	Buona fortuna!	*BWO-na for-TOO-na!*
luggage	bagaglio	*ba-GAHL-yo*
lunch	seconda colazione (f)	*seh-KOHN-da ko-lahts-YO-neh*

M

machine	macchina	*MAHK-kee-na*
madam	signora	*seen-YO-ra*
made	fatto	*FAHT-toh*
maid	domestica	*doh-MESS-tee-ka*
mailbox	buca della posta	*BOO-ka DEL-la PO-sta*
(to) make	fare	*FA-reh*
man	uomo	*WO-mo*
men	uomini	*WO-mee-nee*
manager	amministratore (m)	*ahm-mee-nee-stra-TOH-reh*
many	molti	*MOHL-tee*
map	mappa	*MAHP-pa*
March (month)	marzo	*MART-so*
market	mercato	*mair-KA-toh*
married	sposato	*spo-ZA-toh*
Mass (religious)	messa	*MESS-sa*
matches	fiammiferi	*f'yahm-MEE-feh-ree*

May (month)	maggio	*MAHD-jo*
maybe	forse	*FOR-seh*
May I?	Posso?	*POHS-so?*
me	me, mi	*meh, mee*
(to) mean	voler dire	*vo-LAIR DEE-reh*
meat	carne (f)	*KAR-neh*
mechanic	meccanico	*mek-KA-nee-ko*
medicine	medicina	*meh-dee-CHEE-na*
Mediterranean	Mediterraneo	*meh-dee-tair-RA-neh-yo*
(to) meet (encounter)	incontrare	*een-kohn-TRA-reh*
meeting	riunione (f)	*ree-oon-YO-neh*
member	membro	*MEM-bro*
(to) mend	accomodare	*ahk-ko-mo-DA-reh*
men's room	toeletta	*toh-eh-LET-ta*
menu	lista	*LEES-ta*
message	messaggio	*mehs-SAHD-jo*
meter	metro	*MEH-tro*
Mexico	Messico	*MEHS-see-ko*
(in the) middle	in mezzo	*een MEHD-dzo*
milk	latte (f)	*LAHT-teh*
million	milione (m)	*meel-YO-neh*
mine (See "my.")		
mineral water	acqua minerale (f)	*AH-kwa mee-neh-RA-leh*

minister	ministro	*mee-NEES-tro*
minute	minuto	*mee-NOO-toh*
Miss	signorina	*seen-yo-REE-na*
(to) miss (a train)	perdere	*PAIR-deh-reh*
(to) miss (someone)	sbagliare	*sbahl-YA-reh*
mistake	errore (m)	*air-RO-reh*
Mr.	signore	*seen-YO-reh*
Mrs.	signora	*seen-YO-ra*
misunderstanding	malinteso	*ma-leen-TEH-zo*
model	modello	*mo-DEL-lo*
modern	moderno	*mo-DAIR-no*
moment	momento	*mo-MEN-toh*
Monday	luendì	*loo-neh-DEE*
money	danaro	*da-NA-ro*
monkey	scimmia	*SHEEM-m'ya*
month	mese (m)	*MEH-zeh*
monument	monumento	*mo-noo-MEN-toh*
moon	luna	*LOO-na*
more	più	*p'yoo*
morning	mattino	*maht-TEE-no*
mosquito	zanzara	*DZAN-dza-ra*
most of . . .	la maggior parte di . . .	*la mahd-JOR PAR-teh dee . . .*
(the) most	il più	*eel p'yoo*
mother	madre (f)	*MA-dreh*
mother-in-law	suocera	*SWO-cheh-ra*
motor	motore (m)	*mo-TOH-reh*

motorcycle	motocicletta	*mo-toh-chee-KLET-ta*
mountain	montagna	*mohn-TAHN-ya*
mouse	topo	*TOH-po*
mouth	bocca	*BOHK-ka*
movie	pellicola	*pel-LEE-ko-la*
movies	cinema	*CHEE-neh-ma*
much	molto	*MOHL-toh*
museum	museo	*moo-ZEH-oh*
music	musica	*MOO-zee-ka*
musician	musicista (m)	*moo-zee-CHEES-ta*
must	dovere	*doh-VEH-reh*

(See use on page 78.)

mustache	baffi (m pl)	*BAHF-fee*
mustard	mostarda	*mo-STAR-da*
my, mine	il mio, la mia, i miei, le mie	*eel MEE-yo, la MEE-ya, ee m'yay, leh MEE-eh*

N

name	nome (m)	*NO-meh*
napkin	tovagliolo	*to-vahl-YO-lo*
narcotics	narcotici	*nar-KO-tee-chee*
narrow	stretto	*STRET-toh*

navy	marina	*ma-REE-na*
near	vicino	*vee-CHEE-no*
necessary	necessario	*neh-chess-SAR-yo*
neck	collo	*KOHL-lo*
necktie	cravatta	*kra-VAHT-ta*
(to) need	aver bisogno (di)	*ah-VAIR bee-ZOHN-yo (dee)*
neighborhood	vicinato	*vee-chee-NA-toh*
nephew	nipote (m)	*nee-PO-teh*
nervous	nervoso	*nair-VO-zo*
neutral	neutrale	*neh-oo-TRA-leh*
never	mai	*my*
Never mind.	Non importa.	*nohn eem-POR-ta.*
new	nuovo	*NWO-vo*
news	notizie (f pl)	*no-TEETS-yeh*
newspaper	giornale (m)	*jor-NA-leh*
next	prossimo	*PROHS-see-mo*
nice	gentile	*jen-TEE-leh*
niece	nipote (f)	*nee-PO-teh*
night	notte (f)	*NOHT-teh*
nightclub	locale notturno	*lo-KA-leh noht-TOOR-no*
nightgown	camicia da notte	*ka-MEE-cha da NOHT-teh*
nine	nove	*NO-veh*
nineteen	diciannove	*dee-chahn-NO-veh*
ninety	novanta	*no-VAHN-ta*

no	no	*no*
nobody	nessuno	*nehs-SOO-no*
noise	rumore (m)	*roo-MO-reh*
none (of them)	nessuno	*nehs-SOO-no*
noon	mezzogiorno	*MED-dzo-JOR-no*
normal	normale	*nor-MA-leh*
north	nord (m)	*nord*
nose	naso	*NA-zo*
not	non	*nohn*
Not yet.	Non ancora.	*nohn ahn-KO-ra.*
nothing	niente	*N'YEN-teh*
(to) notice	notare	*no-TA-reh*
noun	nome (m)	*NO-meh*
November	novembre	*no-VEM-breh*
now	adesso	*ah-DESS-so*
nowhere	in nessun posto	*een nes-SOON PO-sto*
number	numero	*NOO-meh-ro*
nurse	infermiera	*een-fairm-YEH-ra*
nuts	noci (m pl)	*NO-che*

O

occasionally	qualche volta	*KWAHL-keh VOHL-ta*
occupied	occupato	*ohk-koo-PA-toh*
ocean	oceano	*oh-CHEH-ah-no*

o'clock

(No exact equivalent; see page 25.)

October	ottobre	*oht-TOH-breh*
of	di	*dee*
(to) offer	offrire	*ohf-FREE-reh*
office	ufficio	*oof-FEE-cho*
officer	ufficiale (m)	*oof-fee-CHA-leh*
often	spesso	*SPEHS-so*
oil	olio	*OHL-yo*
O.K.	va bene	*va BEH-neh*
old	vecchio	*VEK-k'yo*
olive	oliva	*oh-LEE-va*
omelet	frittata	*freet-TA-ta*
on	su	*soo*
once	una volta	*OO-na VOHL-ta*
At once!	Subito!	*SOO-bee-toh!*
one	uno	*OO-no*
one way	senso unico	*SEN-so OO-nee-ko*
onion	cipolla	*chee-POHL-la*
only	solo	*SO-lo*
on time	puntuale	*poon-TWA-leh*
onto	sopra	*SO-pra*
open	aperto	*ah-PAIR-toh*
(to) open	aprire	*ah-PREE-reh*
opera	opera	*OH-peh-ra*
opinion	opinione (f)	*oh-peen-YO-neh*
opportunity	opportunità	*ohp-por-too-nee-TA*

opposite	davanti	*da-VAHN-tee*
or	o	*oh*
orange	arancia	*ah-RAHN-cha*
orchestra	orchestra	*or-KESS-tra*
order	ordine (m)	*OR-dee-neh*
in order to	per (followed by the infinitive)	*pair*
(to) order	ordinare	*or-dee-NA-reh*
original	originale	*oh-ree-jee-NAHL-leh*
other	altro	*AHL-tro*
ought to (See "should.")		
our, ours	nostro, la nostra, i nostri, le nostre	*NOHS-tro, la NOHS-tra, ee NOHS-tree, leh NOHS-treh*
outside	fuori	*FWO-ree*
over	sopra	*SO-pra*
overcoat	cappotto	*kahp-POHT-toh*
over there	laggiù	*lahd-JOO*
overweight (baggage)	peso in più	*PEH-zo een p'yoo*
(to) owe	dovere	*doh-VEH-reh*
own	proprio	*PRO-pr'yo*
owner	proprietario	*pro-pree-yeh-TAR-yo*
ox	bue (m)	*bweh*
oyster	ostriche	*OHS-tree-keh*

P

package	pacco	*PAHK-ko*
paid	pagato	*pa-GA-toh*
pain	dolore (m)	*doh-LO-reh*
(to) paint	dipingere	*dee-PEEN-jeh-reh*
painted	dipinto	*dee-PEEN-toh*
painting	quadro	*KWA-dro*
palace	palazzo	*pa-LAHT-tso*
pan	pentola	*PEN-toh-la*
paper	carta	*KAR-ta*
parade	corteo	*kor-TEH-oh*
Pardon me!	Mi scusi!	*mee SKOO-zee!*
park	parco	*PAR-ko*
(to) park	parcheggiare	*par-ked-JA-reh*
parents	genitori	*jeh-nee-TOH-ree*
part	parte (f)	*PAR-teh*
participate	participio	*par-tee-CHEEP-yo*
partner	socio	*SO-cho*
party	festa	*FESS-ta*
passenger	passeggiero	*pahs-sed-JEH-ro*
passport	passaporto	*pahs-sa-POR-toh*
past	passato	*pahs-SA-toh*
(to) pay	pagare	*pa-GA-reh*
peace	pace (f)	*PA-cheh*
pen	penna	*PEN-na*
pencil	matita	*ma-TEE-ta*

people	gente (f)	*JEN-teh*
percent	percento	*pair-CHEN-toh*
perfect	perfetto	*pair-FET-toh*
perfume	profumo	*pro-FOO-mo*
perhaps	forse	*FOR-seh*
permanent	permanente	*pair-ma-NEN-teh*
permitted	permesso	*pair-MESS-so*
person	persona	*pair-SO-na*
photo	fotografia	*fo-toh-gra-FEE-ya*
piano	piano	*P'YA-no*
picture	quadro	*KWA-dro*
piece	pezzo	*PET-tso*
pier	molo	*MO-lo*
pill	pastiglia	*pa-STEEL-ya*
pillow	cuscino	*koo-SHEE-no*
pin	spillo	*SPEEL-lo*
pink	rosa	*RO-za*
pipe	pipa	*PEE-pa*
pistol	pistola	*pees-TOH-la*
place	posto	*PO-sto*
plain (simple)	semplice	*SEM-plee-cheh*
plan	piano	*P'YA-no*
plane	aereo	*ah-EH-reh-yo*
planet	pianeta	*p'ya-NEH-ta*
plant (garden)	pianta	*P'YAHN-ta*
plant (factory)	impianto	*eem-P'YAHN-toh*
plate	piatto	*P'YAHT-toh*

play (theater)	commedia	*kohm-MED-ya*
(to) play	giocare	*jo-KA-reh*
plastic	plastica	*PLAHS-tee-ka*
pleasant	piacevole	*p'ya-CHEH-vo-leh*
please	prego	*PREH-go*
pleasure	piacere (m)	*p'ya-CHEH-reh*
plural	plurale	*ploo-RA-leh*
pocket	tasca	*TA-ska*
poetry	poesia	*po-eh-ZEE-ya*
(to) point	puntare	*poon-TA-reh*
poisonous	velenoso	*veh-leh-NO-zo*
police	polizia	*po-leet-SEE-ya*
policeman	poliziotto	*po-leets-YOHT-toh*
police station	ufficio di polizia	*oo-FEE-cho dee po-leet-SEE-ya*
polite	educato	*eh-doo-KA-toh*
pool	piscina	*pee-SHEE-na*
poor	povero	*PO-veh-ro*
pope	papa (m)	*PA-pa*
popular	popolare	*po-po-LA-reh*
pork	maiale (m)	*ma-YA-leh*
port	porto	*POR-toh*
Portugal	Portogallo	*port-toh-GAHL-lo*
possible	possibile	*pohs-SEE-bee-leh*
postcard	cartolina	*kar-toh-LEE-na*
post office	posta	*PO-sta*
potato	patata	*pa-TA-ta*

pound	libbra	*LEEB-bra*
(to) practice	esercitare	*eh-sair-chee-TA-reh*
(to) prefer	preferire	*preh-feh-REE-reh*
pregnant	incinta	*een-CHEEN-ta*
(to) prepare	preparare	*preh-pa-RA-reh*
present (gift)	regalo	*reh-GA-lo*
president	presidente	*preh-zee-DEN-teh*
(to) press (clothes)	stirare	*stee-RA-reh*
pretty	grazioso	*grahts-YO-zo*
(to) prevent	prevenire	*preh-veh-NEE-reh*
price	prezzo	*PREHT-tso*
priest	prete (m)	*PREH-teh*
prince	principe (m)	*PREEN-chee-peh*
princess	principessa	*preen-chee-PEHS-sa*
principal	principale	*preen-chee-PA-leh*
prison	prigione (f)	*pree-JO-neh*
private	privato	*pree-VA-toh*
probably	probabilmente	*pro-ba-beel-MEN-teh*
problem	problema (m)	*pro-BLEH-ma*
production	produzione (f)	*pro-doots-YO-neh*
profession	professione (f)	*pro-fess-S'YO-neh*
professor	professore (m)	*pro-fess-SO-reh*
profit	profitto	*pro-FEET-toh*
program	programma (m)	*pro-GRAHM-ma*
(to) promise	promettere	*pro-MET-teh-reh*
promised	promesso	*pro-MESS-so*

pronoun	pronome (m)	*pro-NO-meh*
propaganda	propaganda	*pro-pa-GAHN-da*
property	proprietà	*pro-pree-yeh-TA*
Protestant	protestante	*pro-tehs-TAHN-teh*
public	pubblico	*POOB-blee-ko*
publicity	pubblicità	*poob-blee-chee-TA*
publisher	editore (m)	*eh-dee-TOH-reh*
(to) pull	tirare	*tee-RA-reh*
pure	puro	*POO-ro*
(to) purchase	comprare	*kohm-PRA-reh*
purple	viola	*V'YO-la*
purse	borsa	*BOR-sa*
(to) push	spingere	*SPEEN-jeh-reh*
(to) put	mettere	*MET-teh-reh*
(to) put on	indossare	*een-dohs-SA-reh*

Q

quality	qualità	*kwa-lee-TA*
queen	regina	*reh-JEE-na*
question	domanda	*doh-MAHN-da*
quick	veloce	*veh-LO-cheh*
quickly	presto	*PRESS-toh*
quiet	quieto	*KW'YEH-toh*
quite	*proprio*	*PRO-pree-yo*

R

rabbi	rabbino	*rahb-BEE-no*
rabbit	coniglio	*ko-NEEL-yo*
race (contest)	gara	*GA-ra*
radio	radio	*RAHD-yo*
railroad	ferrovia	*fair-ro-VEE-ya*
rain	pioggia	*P'YOHD-ja*
(It's) raining.	Piove.	*P'YO-veh.*
raincoat	impermeabile	*eem-pair-meh-AH-bee-leh*
rapidly	rapidamente	*ra-pee-da-MEN-teh*
rarely	raramente	*ra-ra-MEN-teh*
rate	rata	*RA-ta*
rather	piuttosto	*p'yoot-TOHS-toh*
razor	rasoio	*ra-ZOY-yo*
(to) read	leggere	*LED-jeh-reh*
read (past part.)	letto	*LET-toh*
ready	pronto	*PROHN-toh*
really	veramente	*veh-ra-MEN-teh*
reason	ragione (f)	*ra-JO-neh*
receipt	ricevuta	*ree-cheh-VOO-ta*
(to) receive	ricevere	*ree-CHEH-veh-reh*
recently	recentemente	*reh-chen-teh-MEN-teh*
recipe	ricetta	*ree-CHET-ta*
(to) recognize	riconoscere	*ree-ko-NO-sheh-reh*

(to) recommend	raccomandare	*rahk-ko-mahn-DA-reh*
red	rosso	*ROHS-so*
refrigerator	frigorifero	*free-go-REE-feh-ro*
(to) refuse	rifiutare	*reef-yoo-TA-reh*
(my) regards to _____	Saluti a _____	*so-LOO-tee ah _____*
regular	regolare	*reh-go-LA-reh*
religion	religione (f)	*reh-lee-JO-neh*
(to) remain	rimanere	*ree-ma-NEH-reh*
(to) remember	ricordare	*ree-kor-DA-reh*
(to) rent	affittare	*ahf-fee-TA-reh*
(to) repair	riparare	*ree-pa-RA-reh*
(to) repeat	ripetere	*ree-PEH-teh-reh*
Repeat, please!	Ripeta, prego!	*ree-PEH-ta, PREH-go!*
report	resoconto	*reh-zo-KOHN-toh*
(to) represent	rappresentare	*rahp-preh-sen-TA-reh*
representative	rappresentante (m or f)	*rahp-preh-sen-TAHN-teh*
responsible	responsabile	*reh-spohn-SA-bee-leh*
resident	residente (m)	*reh-see-DEN-teh*
rest (remainder)	resto	*RESS-toh*
(to) rest	riposare	*ree-po-SA-reh*
restaurant	ristorante (m)	*ree-sto-RAHN-teh*
restroom	toeletta	*toh-eh-LET-ta*

(to) return (come back)	ritornare	*ree-tor-NA-reh*
(to) return (give back)	restituire	*reh-stee-too-EE-reh*
revolution	rivoluzione (f)	*ree-vo-loots-YO-neh*
reward	ricompensa	*ree-kohm-PEN-sa*
rice	riso	*REE-zo*
rich	ricco	*REEK-ko*
(to) ride	andare a	*ahn-DA-reh ah*
right (not left)	destro	*DESS-tro*
right (correct)	giusto	*JOO-sto*
Right away!	Subito!	*SOO-bee-toh!*
ring	anello	*ah-NEL-lo*
riot	rivolta	*ree-VOHL-ta*
river	fiume (m)	*F'YOO-meh*
road	strada	*STRA-da*
roof	tetto	*TET-toh*
room	stanza	*STAHNT-sa*
room service	servizio d'al-bergo (m)	*sehr-VEETS-yo dahl-BAIR-go*
round trip	andata e ritorno	*ahn-DA-ta eh ree-TOR-no*
rug	tappeto	*tahp-PEH-toh*
(to) run	correre	*KOR-reh-reh*
Run!	Corra!	*KOR-ra!*
Russia	Russia	*ROOS-s'ya*
Russian	Russo	*ROOS-so*

S

sad	triste	*TREES-teh*
safe (adj)	salvo	*SAHL-vo*
said	detto	*DET-toh*
sailor	marinaio	*ma-ree-NA-yo*
saint	santo (m), santa (f), san (before a masculine name)	*SAHN-toh, SAHN-ta, sahn*
salad	insalata	*een-sa-LA-ta*
salary	stipendio	*stee-PEND-yo*
sale	vendita	*VEN-dee-ta*
same	stesso	*STEHS-so*
sandwich	panino	*pa-NEE-no*
Saturday	sabato	*SA-ba-toh*
(to) say	dire	*DEE-reh*
scenery	paesaggio	*pye-SAHD-jo*
school	scuola	*SKWO-la*
scissors	forbici	*FOR-bee-chee*
Scotch	scozzese	*skoht-TSEH-zeh*
Scotland	Scozia	*SKOHTS-ya*
sea	mare (m)	*MA-reh*
season	stagione (f)	*sta-JO-neh*
seat	sedile (m)	*seh-DEE-leh*
secretary	segretario (m), -a (f)	*seg-reh-TAR-yo, -ya*
(to) see	vedere	*veh-DEH-reh*

(to) seem	sembrare	*sem-BRA-reh*
It seems . . .	Sembra . . .	*SEM-bra . . .*
seen	visto	*VEES-to*
seldom	raramente	*ra-ra-MEN-teh*
(to) sell	vendere	*VEN-deh-reh*
(to) send	mandare	*mahn-DA-reh*
(to) send for	richiedere	*ree-K'YEH-deh-reh*
September	settembre	*set-TEM-breh*
serious	serio	*SAIR-yo*
service	servizio	*sair-VEETS-yo*
seven	sette	*SET-teh*
seventeen	diciassette	*dee-chahs-SET-teh*
seventy	settanta	*set-TAHN-ta*
several	parecchi	*pa-REK-kee*
shark	pescecane (m)	*peh-sheh-KA-neh*
sharp	affilato	*ahf-fee-LA-toh*
she	essa	*ESS-sa*
ship	nave (f)	*NA-veh*
shipment	spedizione (f)	*speh-deet-S'YO-neh*
shirt	camicia	*ka-MEE-cha*
shop	negozio	*neh-GOHTS-yo*
short	corto	*KOR-toh*
(I) should	dovrei	*dohv-RAY*
you (sg), he, she should	dovrebbe	*dohv-REB-beh*
we should	dovremmo	*dohv-REM-mo*
you (pl), they should	dovrebbero	*dohv-REB-beh-ro*

shoulder	spalla	*SPAHL-la*
show	spettacolo	*spet-TA-ko-lo*
(to) show	mostrare	*mo-STRA-reh*
Show me!	Mi mostri!	*mee MO-stree!*
shower	doccia	*DOHT-cha*
shrimps	scampi (m)	*SKAHM-pee*
shut	chiuso	*K'YOO-zo*
(to) shut	chiudere	*K'YOO-deh-reh*
Sicilian	siciliano	*see-cheel-YA-no*
sick	ammalato	*ahm-ma-LA-toh*
(to) sign	firmare	*feer-MA-reh*
silk	seta	*SEH-ta*
silver	argento	*ar-JEN-toh*
since	da	*da*
sincerely	sinceramente	*seen-cheh-ra-MEN-teh*
(to) sing	cantare	*kahn-TA-reh*
singer	cantante (m, f)	*kahn-TAHN-teh*
sir	signore	*seen-YO-reh*
sister	sorella	*so-REL-la*
sister-in-law	cognata	*kohn-YA-ta*
(Please) sit down.	Si accomodi.	*see ahk-KO-mo-dee.*
six	sei	*say*
sixteen	sedici	*SEH-dee-chee*
sixty	sessanta	*sehs-SAHN-ta*
size	misura	*mee-ZOO-ra*
(to) skate	pattinare	*paht-tee-NA-reh*

(to) ski	sciare	*shee-AH-reh*
skirt	gonna	*GOHN-na*
sky	cielo	*CHEH-lo*
(to) sleep	dormire	*dor-MEE-reh*
sleeve	manica	*MA-nee-ka*
slowly	lentamente	*len-ta-MEN-teh*
small	piccolo	*PEEK-ko-lo*
(to) smoke	fumare	*foo-MA-reh*
snow	neve (f)	*NEH-veh*
so	così	*ko-ZEE*
soap	sapone (m)	*sa-PO-neh*
sock	calzetto	*kahld-ZET-toh*
sofa	divano	*dee-VA-no*
soft	soffice	*SOHF-fee-cheh*
soldier	soldato	*sohl-DA-toh*
some (a little)	un po'	*oon po*
some (more than one)	alcuni	*ahl-KOO-nee*
somebody	qualcuno	*kwahl-KOO-no*
something	qualcosa	*kwahl-KO-za*
something else	qualcos'altro	*kwahl-ko-ZAHL-tro*
sometimes	qualche volta	*kwahl-keh VOHL-ta*
somewhere	in qualche posto	*een KWAHL-keh PO-sto*
son	figlio	*FEEL-yo*
son-in-law	genero	*JEN-eh-ro*

song	canzone (f)	*kahnt-SO-neh*
soon	presto	*PRESS-toh*
soprano	soprano	*sop-PRA-no*
(I am) sorry.	Mi scusi.	*mee SKOO-zee.*
soup	minestra	*mee-NESS-tra*
south	sud (m)	*sood*
South America	Sud America	*sood ah-MEH-ree-ka*
South American	sudamericano	*sood-ah-meh-ree-KA-no*
souvenir	ricordo	*ree-KOR-doh*
Spain	Spagna	*SPAHN-ya*
Spanish	spagnolo	*spahn-YO-lo*
(to) speak	parlare	*par-LA-reh*
special	speciale	*speh-CHA-leh*
(to) spend	spendere	*SPEN-deh-reh*
spoon	cucchiaio	*kook-K'YA-yo*
sport	sport (m)	*sport*
spring (season)	primavera	*pree-ma-VER-ra*
stairs	scale (f, pl)	*SKA-leh*
stamp	francobollo	*frahn-ko-BOHL-lo*
star	stella	*STEL-la*
(to) start	cominciare	*ko-meen-CHA-reh*
state	stato	*STA-toh*
station	stazione	*stahts-YO-neh*
statue	statua	*STA-too-ah*
(to) stay	stare	*STA-reh*
steak	bistecca	*bees-TEHK-ka*

steel	ferro	*FAIR-ro*
still (adv)	ancora	*ahn-KO-ra*
stocking	calza	*KAHLD-za*
stone	sasso	*SAHS-so*
Stop!	Si fermi!	*see FAIR-mee!*
Stop it!	La smetta!	*la SMET-ta!*
store	negozio	*neh-GOHTS-yo*
storm	temporale (m)	*tem-po-RA-leh*
story	storia	*STOR-ya*
straight	diritto	*dee-REET-toh*
straight ahead	avanti diritto	*ah-VAHN-tee dee-REET-toh*
strange	strano	*STRA-no*
street	strada	*STRA-da*
string	corda	*KOR-da*
strong	forte	*FOR-teh*
student	studente (m or f)	*stoo-DEN-teh*
(to) study	studiare	*stoo-D'YA-reh*
style	stile (m)	*STEE-leh*
subway	metropolitana	*meh-tro-po-lee-TA-na*
suddenly	improvvisamente	*eem-prohv-vee-za-MEN-teh*
sugar	zucchero	*DZOOK-keh-ro*
suit	vestito	*ves-TEE-toh*
suitcase	valigia	*va-LEE-ja*
summer	estate (f)	*es-TA-teh*
sun	sole (m)	*SO-leh*

Sunday	domenica	*do-MEH-nee-ka*
sure	sicuro	*see-KOO-ro*
surely	sicuramente	*see-koo-ra-MEN-teh*
surprise	sorpresa	*sor-PREH-za*
sweater	maglione	*mahl-YO-neh*
sweet	dolce	*DOHL-cheh*
(to) swim	nuotare	*nwo-TA-reh*
swimming pool	piscina	*pee-SHEE-na*
Swiss	svizzero	*ZVEET-tseh-ro*
Switzerland	Svizzera	*ZVEET-tseh-ra*

T

table	tavola	*TA-vo-la*
tablecloth	tovaglia	*toh-VAHL-ya*
tailor	sarto	*SAR-toh*
(to) take	prendere	*PREN-deh-reh*
(to) take away	ritirare	*ree-tee-RA-reh*
(to) take a walk, take a ride	passeggiare	*pahs-sed-JA-reh*
(to) talk	parlare	*par-LA-reh*
tall	alto	*AHL-toh*
tank	serbatoio	*ser-ba-TOY-yo*
tape	nastro	*NA-stro*
tape recorder	registratore	*reh-jee-stra-TOH-reh*

tax	tassa	*TAHS-sa*
taxi	tassì (m)	*tahs-SEE*
tea	tè (m)	*teh*
(to) teach	insegnare	*een-sehn-YA-reh*
teacher	insegnante (m or f)	*een-sen-YAHN-teh*
team	squadra	*SKWA-dra*
telegram	telegramma (m)	*teh-leh-GRAHM-ma*
telephone	telefono	*teh-LEH-fo-no*
television	televisione (f)	*teh-leh-vees-YO-neh*
(to) tell	dire	*DEE-reh*
Tell him (her) that . . .	Gli (le) dica che . . .	*l'yee (leh) DEE-ka keh . . .*
temperature	temperatura	*tem-peh-ra-TOO-ra*
ten	dieci	*D'YEH-chee*
tenor	tenore (m)	*teh-NO-reh*
terrace	terrazza	*tair-RAHT-tsa*
terrible	terribile	*tair-REE-bee-leh*
than	che	*keh*
thank you	grazie	*GRAHTS-yeh*
that (pron)	quello	*KWEL-lo*
that (conj)	che	*keh*
the	il, la	*eel, la* (See the introduction to dictionary.)
theater	teatro	*teh-AH-tro*
their, theirs	il loro, la loro, i loro, le loro	*eel (la, ee, leh) LO-ro*

them	li (m), le (f), loro	*lee, leh, LO-ro*
then	allora	*ahl-LO-ra*
there	là	*la*
there is . . .	c'è . . .	*cheh . . .*
there are . . .	ci sono . . .	*chee SO-no . . .*
these (adj)	questi	*KWESS-tee*
they	essi (m), esse (f)	*ESS-see, ESS-seh*
thin	magro	*MA-gro*
thing	cosa	*KO-za*
(to) think	pensare	*pen-SA-reh*
Do you think that . . . ?	Pensa che . . . ?	*PEN-sa keh . . . ?*
third	terzo	*TAIRT-so*
thirteen	tredici	*TREH-dee-chee*
thirty	trenta	*TRAIN-ta*
this	questo	*KWESS-toh*
those	quelli	*KWEL-lee*
thousand	mille	*MEEL-leh*
thread	filo	*FEE-lo*
three	tre	*treh*
throat	gola	*GO-la*
through	attraverso	*aht-tra-VAIR-so*
Thursday	giovedì	*jo-veh-DEE*
ticket	biglietto	*beel-YET-toh*
tie	cravatta	*kra-VAHT-ta*
tiger	tigre (m)	*TEE-greh*
time	ora	*OH-ra*

tip	mancia	*MAHN-cha*
tire	pneumatico	*p'neh-oo-MA-tee-ko*
tired	stanco	*STAHN-ko*
to (direction)	a	*ah*
to (in order to)	per	*pair*
toast	pane tostato	*PA-neh toh-STA-toh*
tobacco	tabacco	*ta-BAHK-ko*
today	oggi	*OHD-jee*
toe	dito del piede	*DEE-toh del P'YEH-deh*
together	insieme	*eens-YEH-meh*
tomato	pomodoro	*po-mo-DOH-ro*
tomb	tomba	*TOHM-ba*
tongue	lingua	*LEEN-gwa*
tonight	stanotte	*sta-NOHT-teh*
too (also)	anche	*AHN-keh*
too (excessive)	troppo	*TROHP-po*
tool	strumento	*stroo-MEN-toh*
tooth	dente (m)	*DEN-teh*
toothbrush	spazzolino da denti	*spaht-tso-LEE-no da DEN-tee*
toothpaste	dentifricio	*den-tee-FREE-cho*
tour	giro	*JEE-ro*
tourist	turista	*too-REES-ta*
toward	verso	*VAIR-so*
towel	asciugamano	*ah-shoo-ga-MA-no*

tower	torre (f)	*TOHR-reh*
town	città	*cheet-TA*
toy	giocattolo	*jo-KAHT-toh-lo*
traffic	traffico	*TRAHF-fee-ko*
train	treno	*TREH-no*
translation	traduzione	*tra-doots-YO-neh*
(to) travel	viaggiare	*v'yahd-JA-reh*
travel agent	agente di viaggio	*ah-JEN-teh dee V'YAHD-jo*
traveler	viaggiatore	*v'yahd-ja-TOH-reh*
treasurer	tesoriere	*teh-zor-YEH-reh*
tree	albero	*AHL-beh-ro*
trip	viaggio	*V'YAHD-jo*
trouble	disturbo	*dee-STOOR-bo*
trousers	pantaloni (m pl)	*pahn-ta-LO-nee*
truck	camion (m)	*KAHM-yohn*
true	vero	*VEH-ro*
truth	verità	*veh-ree-TA*
(to) try	provare	*pro-VA-reh*
(to) try on	indossare	*een-dohs-SA-reh*
Tuesday	martedì	*mar-teh-DEE*
Turkey	Turchia	*toor-KEE-ya*
Turkish	turco	*TOOR-ko*
(to) turn	girare	*jee-RA-reh*
(to) turn off	spegnere	*SPEN-yeh-reh*
(to) turn on	accendere	*aht-CHEN-deh-reh*
twelve	dodici	*DOH-dee-chee*

two	due	*DOO-weh*
typewriter	macchina da scrivere	*MAHK-kee na da SKREE-veh-reh*
typical	tipico	*TEE-pee-ko*

U

ugly	brutto	*BROOT-toh*
umbrella	ombrello	*ohm-BREL-lo*
uncle	zio	*DZEE-oh*
under	sotto	*SOHT-toh*
(to) understand	capire	*ka-PEE-reh*
Do you understand?	Capisce?	*ka-PEE-sheh?*
I don't understand.	Non capisco.	*nohn ka-PEES-ko.*
understood	capito	*ka-PEE-toh*
underwear	biancheria personale	*b'yahn-keh-REE-ah pair-so-NA-leh*
unfortunately	sfortunatamente	*sfor-too-na-ta-MEN-teh*
uniform	uniforme (m)	*oo-nee-FOR-meh*
United States	Stati Uniti	*STA-tee oo-NEE-tee*
United Nations	Nazioni Unite	*nahdz-YO-nee oo-NEE-teh*
university	università	*oo-nee-vair-see-TA*
until	fino	*FEE-no*

up	su	*soo*
urgent	urgente	*oor-JEN-teh*
us (object)	ci	*chee*
us (with prep)	noi	*noy*
(to) use	usare	*oo-ZA-reh*
used to (in the habit of)	abituato a	*ah-beet-WA-toh ah*
useful	utile	*OO-tee-leh*
usually	di solito	*dee SO-lee-toh*

V

vacant	libero	*LEE-beh-ro*
vacation	vacanza	*va-KAHN-dza*
vaccination	vaccino	*vaht-CHEE-no*
valley	valle (f)	*VAHL-leh*
valuable	di valore	*dee va-LO-reh*
value	valore	*va-LO-reh*
vanilla	vaniglia	*va-NEEL-ay*
various	vario	*VAR-yo*
veal	vitello	*vee-TEL-lo*
vegetable	verdura	*vair-DOO-ra*
verb	verbo	*VAIR-bo*
very	molto	*MOHL-toh*
very well	molto bene	*MOHL-toh BEH-neh*
view	vista	*VEES-ta*

village	villaggio	*veel-LAHD-jo*
vinegar	aceto	*ah-CHEH-toh*
visa	visto	*VEES-toh*
visit	visita	*vee-ZEE-ta*
(to) visit	visitare	*vee-zee-TA-reh*
violin	violion	*vee-yo-LEE-no*
vivid	vivido	*VEE-vee-doh*
voice	voce (f)	*VO-cheh*
volcano	vulcano	*vool-KA-no*
voyage	viaggio	*V'YAHD-jo*

W

waist	vita	*VEE-ta*
(to) wait	aspettare	*ah-spet-TA-reh*
Wait here!	Aspetti qui!	*ah-SPET-tee kwee!*
waiter	cameriere	*ka-mair-YEH-reh*
waitress	cameriera	*ka-mair-YEH-ra*
(to) walk	camminare	*kahm-mee-NA-reh*
wall	muro	*MOO-ro*
wallet	portafoglio	*por-ta-FOHL-yo*
(to) want	volere	*vo-LEH-reh*
I want	voglio	*VOHL-yo*
you (sg) **want**	Lei vuole	*lay VWO-leh*
he, she wants	vuole	*VWO-leh*
we want	vogliamo	*vohl-YA-mo*

you (pl) **want**	Loro vogliono	*LO-ro VOHL-yo-no*
they want	vogliono	*VOHL-yo-no*
Do you want . . . ?	Vuole . . . ?	*VWO-leh . . . ?*
Does he (she) want . . . ?	Vuole . . . ?	*VWO-leh . . . ?*
war	guerra	*GWAIR-ra*
warm	caldo	*KAHL-doh*
was		
I was	ero	*EH-ro*
he, she, it was	era	*EH-ra*
(to) wash	lavare	*la-VA-reh*
watch	orologio	*oh-ro-LO-jo*
Watch out!	Attento!	*aht-TEN-toh!*
water	acqua	*AHK-kwa*
water color	acquerello	*ahk-kweh-REL-lo*
way (manner)	modo	*MO-doh*
way (road)	strada	*STRA-da*
we	noi	*noy*
weak	debole	*DEH-bo-leh*
(to) wear	indossare	*een-dohs-SA-reh*
weather	tempo	*TEM-po*
wedding	matrimonio	*ma-tree-MOHN-yo*
week	settimana	*set-tee-MA-na*
weekend	fine settimana	*FEE-neh set-tee-MA-na*
(to) weigh	pesare	*peh-SA-reh*
weight	peso	*PEH-zo*

Welcome!	Benvenuto!	*ben-ven-NOO-toh!*
You are welcome.	Prego.	*PREH-go.*
well	bene	*BEH-neh*

went

I went	sono andato, -ta	*SO-no ahn-DA-toh, -ta*
you (sg) went	Lei è andato, -ta	*lay eh ahn-DA-toh, -ta*
he, she went	è andato, -ta	*eh ahn-DA-toh, -ta*
we went	siamo andati, -te	*S'YA-mo ahn-DA-tee, - teh*
you (pl) went	Loro sono andati,-te	*LO-ro SO-no ahn-DA-tee, -teh*
they went	sono andati, -te	*SO-no ahn-DA-tee, -teh*

were

you (sg) were	Lei era	*lay EH-ra*
we were	eravamo	*eh-ra-VA-mo*
you (pl) were	Loro erano	*LO-ro EH-ra-no*
they were	erano	*EH-ra-no*
west	ovest	*OH-vest*
what?	cosa?	*KO-za?*
What's the matter?	Cosa è successo?	*KO-za eh soot-CHEHS-so?*
What time is it?	Che ora è?	*keh OH-ra eh?*
What do you want?	Cosa desidera?	*KO-za deh-ZEE-deh-ra?*
wheel	ruota	*R'WO-ta*
when	quando	*KWAHN-doh*

where	dove	*DOH-veh*
Where is . . . ?	Dov'è . . . ?	*doh-VEH . . . ?*
which	quale	*KWA-leh*
while	mentre	*MEN-treh*
white	bianco	*B'YAHN-ko*
who	chi	*kee*
whole	intero	*een-TEH-ro*
whom	chi	*kee*
why?	perchè?	*pair-KEH?*
Why not?	Perchè no?	*pair-KEH no?*
wide	largo	*LAR-go*
widow	vedova	*VEH-doh-va*
widower	vedovo	*VEH-doh-vo*
wife	moglie (f)	*MOHL-yeh*

will: The future is formed by adding one of the following endings, according to the subject, to the stem of the verb. For a verb whose infinitive ends in **-are -ere: (io) -erò, (Lei, egli, ella) -erà, (noi) -eremo, (Loro, essi, esse) -eranno.** For a verb whose infinitive ends in **-ire: (io) -irò, (Lei, egli, ella) -irà, (noi) -iremo, (Loro, essi, esse) -iranno.**

I will speak	parlerò	*par-leh-RO*
he will understand	capirà	*ka-pee-RA*
he won't understand	non capirà	*nohn ka-pee-RA*
(to) win	vincere	*VEEN-cheh-reh*
wind	vento	*VEN-toh*
window	finestra	*fee-NEHS-tra*
wine	vino	*VEE-no*
winter	inverno	*een-VAIR-no*

(to) wish	desiderare	*deh-zee-deh-RA-reh*
without	senza	*SENT-sa*
wolf	lupo	*LOO-po*
woman	donna	*DOHN-na*
wonderful	meraviglioso	*meh-ra-veel-YO-zo*
won't (see "will.")		
wood	legno	*LEN-yo*
woods	bosco	*BOHS-ko*
wool	lana	*LA-na*
word	parola	*pa-RO-la*
work	lavoro	*la-VO-ro*
(to) work	lavorare	*la-vo-RA-reh*
world	mondo	*MOHN-doh*
worried	preoccupato	*preh-ohk-koo-PA-toh*
worse	peggio	*PED-jo*

would: Express the idea of "would" by adding the appropriate one of the following endings to the stem of the verb. For a verb whose infinitive ends in **-are** or **ere: (io) -erei, (Lei, egli, ella) -erebbe, (noi) -eremmo, (Loro, essi, esse) -erebbero**. For a verb whose infinitive ends in **-ire: (io) -irei, (Lei, egli, ella) -irebbe, (noi) -remmo, (Loro, essi, esse) -irebbero**.

I would try	proverei	*pro-veh-RAY*
he would open	aprirebbe	*ah-pree-REB-beh*
I would like	vorrei	*vohr-RAY*
Would you, he, she like . . . ?	Le piacerebbe . . . ?	*leh p'ya-cheh-REB-beh . . . ?*
wrist	polso	*POHL-so*
(to) write	scrivere	*SKREE-veh-reh*

writer	scrittore (m)	*skreet-TOR-reh*
Write it!	Lo scriva!	*lo SKREE-va!*
wrong	sbagliato	*zbahl-YA-toh*

Y

year	anno	*AHN-no*
yellow	giallo	*JAHL-lo*
yes	sì	*see*
yesterday	ieri	*YEH-ree*
yet	ancora	*ahn-KO-ra*

you (See introduction to the dictionary.)

(as subject)	Lei, tu (sg); Loro, voi (pl)	*lay, too, LO-ro, voy*
(as object)	La, ti (sg); Li, vi	*la, tee, lee, vee*
young	giovane	*JO-va-neh*
your, yours (sg)	il Suo, la Sua, i Suoi, le Sue	*eel SOO-wo, la SOO-wa, ee swoy, leh SOO-eh*
your, yours (pl)	il Loro, la Loro, i Loro, le Loro	*eel (la, ee, leh) Lo-ro*
Yugoslavia	Jugoslavia	*yoo-go-SLAHV-ya*

Z

zipper	chiusura lampo	*k'yoo-ZOO-ra LAHM-po*
zone	zona	*DZO-na*
zoo	zoo	*dzo-oh*

POINT TO THE ANSWER

To make sure that you understand the answer to a question, show the following section to the Italian person you are talking to. The sentence in Italian after the arrow asks him to point to the answer to your question.

 La prego di mostrare qui sotto la Sua risposta alla mia domanda. Molte grazie!

Sì.
Yes.

No.
No.

Forse.
Perhaps.

Certamente.
Certainly.

Va bene.
All right.

Mi scusi.
Excuse me.

Capisco.
I understand.

Non capisco.
I don't understand.

Cosa desidera?
What do you want?

Lo so.
I know.

Non lo so.
I don't know.

Ancora.
Again (or) More.

Basta così.
Enough.

Aperto.
Open.

Chiuso.
Closed.

Troppo.
Too much.

Non è sufficiente.
Not enough.

Vietato entrare.
No admittance.

Proibito.
It is forbidden.

Proprietà privata.
Private property.

Lei deve andarsene.
You must leave.

Adesso.	Più tardi.	Troppo presto.
Now.	Later.	Too early.

Troppo tardi.	Oggi.	Domani.	Ieri.
Too late.	Today.	Tomorrow.	Yesterday.

Questa sera.	Ieri sera.	Domani sera.
Tonight.	Last night.	Tomorrow night.

Questa settimana.	La settimana scorsa.
This week.	Last week.

La prossima settimana.	È possibile.	Non è possibile.
Next week.	It's possible.	It's not possible.

D'accordo.	Benissimo.	Non va bene.
It is agreed.	Very good.	It isn't good.

È vicino.	Troppo lontano.	Molto lontano.
It's near.	Too far.	Very far.

Qui.	Là.
Here.	There.

Giri a sinistra.	Giri a destra.
Turn left.	Turn right.

Vada diritto.	Venga con me.
Go straight ahead.	Come with me.

Mi segua.	Andiamo.
Follow me.	Let's go.

Siamo arrivati.	Si fermi qui.	Mi aspetti.
We have arrived.	Stop here.	Wait for me.

Non posso.	Aspetto.	Devo andare.
I cannot.	I will wait.	I must go.

Torni più tardi.	Torno subito.
Come back later.	I'll be right back.

Io mi chiamo _____.
My name is _____.

E lei?
And you?

Il numero di telefono.
Telephone number.

Indirizzo.
Address.

lunedì	**martedì**	**mercoledì**	**giovedì**
Monday	Tuesday	Wednesday	Thursday

venerdì	**sabato**	**domenica**
Friday	Saturday	Sunday

Alle _____.
At _____ o'clock.

Costa _____ **lire.**
It costs _____ lire.

uno	**due**	**tre**	**quattro**	**cinque**
one	two	three	four	five

sei	**sette**	**otto**	**nove**	**dieci**
six	seven	eight	nine	ten

undici	**dodici**	**tredici**	**quattordici**
eleven	twelve	thirteen	fourteen

quindici	**sedici**	**diciassette**	**diciotto**
fifteen	sixteen	seventeen	eighteen

diciannove	**venti**	**trenta**	**quaranta**
nineteen	twenty	thirty	forty

cinquanta	**sessanta**	**settanta**	**ottanta**
fifty	sixty	seventy	eighty

novanta	**cento**
ninety	one hundred

mille	**diecimila**
one thousand	ten thousand